SAGE HALL

Experiments in Coeducation

and Preservation

at Cornell University

Jennifer Cleland

Robert P. Stundtner

© 2011 PhG Publishing, Ithaca, NY

All rights reserved

Printed in the United States of America

Library of Congress Control Number: 2011906279

Cleland, Jennifer, 1951–

Sage Hall: Experiments in Coeducation and Preservation at Cornell University

Cover image: Charles Babcock's architectural drawing of Sage College, "Section, through centre, looking North" June 15, 1872

Courtesy of the Division of Rare and Manuscript Collections, Cornell University Library

Cover design by Jennifer Cleland

for Patrick,

who made us a family

Acknowledgements

We would like to recognize our debt to the historians of Cornell University, whose work provided the material used to assemble the first part of this book; these sources are listed in the bibliography. I refer scholars to the original material for authoritative facts regarding the events and people in this book.

We would also like to thank the staff of the Rare Books and Manuscripts Collection at the Kroch Library at Cornell for their assistance in accessing original documents. We especially appreciate the help of Elaine Engst, University Archivist at Cornell, who was an early reader of our text.

Thanks as well to all those who encouraged us to write the book, and allowed us to use their email messages chronicling the progress of the Sage Hall renovation.

Finally, thanks to our first reader Jean Cleland, for her encouragement and inspiration.

TABLE OF CONTENTS

Introduction..viii

1. The Men Who Built Sage Hall............................1

2. The Woman Question.....................................38

3. The Experiment of Coeducation........................82

4. The Preservation Question.............................130

5. The Transformation of Sage Hall....................192

6. To the Coming Man and Woman....................240

Epilogue..314

Bibliography...319

Authors' Biographies....................................321

INTRODUCTION

By Jennifer Cleland

In the summer of 1967, my mother took me to visit Cornell University as a prospective student. The beautiful campus and the lively atmosphere in the small college town seemed conducive to learning, but in fact the times were such that the campus was partially shut down in the spring semesters of my first two years. College students in good standing were being drafted to fight in the jungles of Vietnam, and the draft lottery of 1969 triggered strong resistance to the government's disastrous foreign policy. Antiwar protests and a takeover of the student union by activists for what would eventually become the Africana Studies and Research Center disrupted the university in the spring of 1969, my freshman year. All this provided a stimulating political and social experience, but sometimes classes were cancelled, replaced by demonstrations and sit-ins, and the carnival that was the 60's counter-culture infringed on academic pursuits for some students, including me.

I took a leave of absence after my junior year, fully intending to return within the five years that it granted me. Instead I embarked on a grand adventure as a founding member of the Highwoods Stringband, a group that played traditional Appalachian music on three continents and received a Grammy

Introduction

nomination for a recording made in Carnegie Hall. My lifestyle as a traveling musician gave way to domesticity in the '80's, and I returned to Ithaca in 1990 with my then 7-year-old son Patrick to pursue a doctorate in Romance Studies. I was happy to come back to a community where I still had friends, and that I felt was a good place to raise a child.

Bob Stundtner joined the Navy in 1968, and spent four years as an electronics technician, first in the Philippines and then on a destroyer escort out of Long Beach, California; on his discharge, he completed a psychology degree at SUNY Oswego in 1976. In 1980, Bob took a position at Cornell as a project coordinator in the Maintenance Management Department, and by 1990 had worked his way up to project management. He led a group of designers and contractors as Cornell's project manager for the controversial transformation of the historic building, Sage Hall, between 1996 and 1998. The building had gone through many changes in the course of its 120 years, as floor plans and even infrastructure were altered to meet new needs and standards. By the time the university was considering allowing the Johnson School to relocate there, Sage Hall was in sad shape.

The building needed the upgrade, but the transformation wasn't easy. The challenges of the project were many, ranging from the unpredictability inherent in all renovations to the difficult upstate New York climate. The main challenge was to get all the

Introduction

pieces to fit together in a timely fashion when contractors were late or the weather didn't allow progress. One of the most exciting incidents featured a brick wall adjacent to the interior courtyard that moved 18" in one day during the asbestos removal!

But even before the project got under way, the innovative design of the renovation, which retained but gutted the historic brick shell and replaced the dilapidated interior with a brand new floor plan, triggered an assessment review of its impact on a historic structure by the city's planning board, and legal challenges to the building permit for the project.

Controversy was not new to Sage Hall, originally built as a residential and dining hall for women students at Cornell. At the inaugural ceremony for the university in 1868, Ezra Cornell, founder of the university, and A.D. White, its first president, had declared their belief in the need for women's education, but also felt that they did not have the facilities to accommodate women students at that time. Henry Sage, an entrepreneur with a fortune made from logging, was a major benefactor of the university, and a staunch supporter of women's right to an education, and proposed to donate funds to build a residence hall expressly for women, as well as an endowment for its maintenance. The funding would be contingent on the admission of women to Cornell University, and also stipulated that "instruction shall be afforded to young women,

Introduction

by the Cornell University, as broad and as thorough as that now afforded to young men."

Sage Residential College for Women opened its doors in 1875, a bold move by the young university since only a few other institutions of higher education in the U.S. admitted women at the time. The building, designed by Charles Babcock, Cornell's first architecture professor, featured state-of-the-art facilities, including a wading pool, gymnasium, botanical conservatory, gas lighting, steam heat and indoor plumbing. Yet the concept of coeducation was not universally embraced by the university community, and the building, while enabling the education of women, also functioned to confine them to a supervised space.

When I entered Cornell University in 1968, women still occupied relatively cloistered, all-female residence halls. The buildings were grouped on the northern edge of the campus (as far from downtown as possible). Unlike the unregulated men's dorms, women had a 10:30 PM curfew that was finally revoked in the spring of 1969. Until then, the rules for women living in Cornell dormitories were about the same as they had been at Sage College at the turn of the 20th century. The disproportion of men to women students at Cornell, 3 to 1, also persisted into the 1960's, and the purported reason for that disparity was still the lack of campus facilities, or "beds," for women.

Introduction

Today, *in loco parentis* is out of style, and male and female students share floors and even bathrooms of residence halls. When the Johnson Graduate School of Management dedicated its new home at Sage Hall, the president of that year's graduating class was a woman – we actually have come a long way.

In August of 1996, I went to a Sunday night Irish session in a bar downtown for the first time. One of the musicians recognized me from my Highwoods days, and invited me to come back and play music with them the next week. Little did I realize that my future husband sat at the other end of the bar that night. Bob was a friend of the session musicians; within a week we had met, and within two months we were dating. We married in 1998, and our early courtship is part of this story. We decided to assemble the project updates that Bob had written periodically to describe the progress of the Sage Hall renovation to the Cornell community, and to weave those reports into the story of our blossoming relationship.

This project is personal in another way. My graduate research drew me into the age-old "woman question," that weighed women's needs and ambitions against society's fear of their threat to the status quo. This debate, a central social issue for my generation, continues into the 21st century. I wanted to put what was viewed in the 19th century as "the experiment" of

Introduction

coeducation into the larger historical context that made Ithaca the place for that experiment to happen.

The Finger Lakes region of New York has been a hotbed of social activism since the Erie Canal opened the western territories to settlement. Elizabeth Cady Stanton and Susan B. Anthony, tireless advocates for women's rights, also shared an upstate New York social environment and sensibility with Ezra Cornell and A.D. White. The optimism and utopianism of the time shaped their lives: each of them took part in the larger project of shaping a new society, and what they believed would be a better future, as human society evolved on its preordained path to perfection. It was the social landscape of upstate New York that made the secular, coeducational institution that is Cornell University a reality.

Sage College and Sage Chapel as seen from McGraw Tower 1875

Courtesy of the Division of Rare and Manuscript Collections,

Cornell University Library

Chapter 1: The Men Who Built Sage Hall

Ezra Cornell, the founder of Cornell University, Andrew D. White, its first president, and Henry Sage, the patron who financed the construction and endowment of Sage Hall, were very different men, but they had the 19th century and upstate New York in common. Their personal experiences and beliefs shaped Cornell University, in particular the coeducational institution that its founders had visualized from the outset. While Cornell, Sage and White disagreed about some tenets of the feminist cause that was emerging in the region, each of them had his own reasons for supporting a woman's right to an education in the 19th century.

Cornell was an unlikely founder of a world-class university, born to neither wealth nor social prestige. The eldest child of Quakers whose ancestors sought religious freedom in America, Ezra was born in 1807 in what is now the Bronx, New York. His father, Elijah, was a potter, and adverse economic conditions in 1818 led the family of eight to decamp to an unworked farm in DeRuyter, New York, northeast of Ithaca. In November and December of that year, the family traveled by covered wagon to their 150 acres on Crum Hill, in an area still known as Quaker Basin. Ezra helped his father build a log house and a kiln, and assisted him with his pottery business; occasionally he attended school in the winter, following a curriculum that led to what would now be considered a fifth grade education.

Ezra embraced the work ethic of his parents, and was a precocious autodidact. Some anecdotes of his youth suggest the native wit and determination that contributed to his eventual achievements. At the age of seventeen, during the construction of a workshop for his father, he noticed a mistake in the design. According to his brother-in-law's memoir, when Ezra pointed it out the boss "foamed with rage, and father reprimanded me for my presumption and impudence. I, however, was not to be put down by angry words, for I knew I was right, and I insisted upon it and at last secured an examination of the subject by some other carpenters who worked on the frame. They saw the error and took sides with me, and the 'boss' had finally to give it up and correct his mistake." In the aftermath of the small-town controversy, the local guild of carpenters even tried to sabotage Ezra's construction of the building. Finally, Ezra's structure was "pronounced by all hands the best one that had ever been raised in the neighborhood. My triumph was so complete on this occasion that my friends mounted me on their shoulders and marched me around the frame in the highest glee of enthusiasm." This youthful sense of self-vindication would serve him well in his future endeavors, when he often pitted his convictions against those of his adversaries.

The Men Who Built Sage Hall

Leaving home at the age of nineteen, Cornell walked from DeRuyter to Ithaca, about thirty miles, looking for work. The fledgling port city on the south end of Cayuga Lake was a gateway to the newly constructed Erie Canal, linking Ithaca to New York City and the east coast as well as to the new western frontier, and profited from the booming trade in lumber and salt.

Cornell found work at Jeremiah Beebe's gypsum and flour mills at the foot of Ithaca Falls, and within a year became the mechanic of the operation. In an engineering feat that seems to defy explanation other than his native intelligence, Ezra built a dam above the falls and blasted a tunnel through the rock to channel the water that powered the mill, replacing an unreliable wooden sluiceway suspended from the top of the falls. The two shafts of the 200-foot long, 15-foot high tunnel met up within a few inches. This accomplishment portended his future success, and in the decades to come, Cornell became a prominent and wealthy citizen of Ithaca.

Ezra married Mary Ann Wood, whose father had a large farm near Etna, in 1831. Judging from a letter that he wrote to his father, this was not anticipated: "I presume you will expect to hear that I have made a wife of Miss Byington, but that ant [sic] the case and I never intended it should be but I am happy to inform you that I am about to form a matrimonial connection with Miss Mary

Ann Wood." Mary Ann was an Episcopalian, and when Ezra was excommunicated by the DeRuyter Society of Friends for "marrying out of meeting," he responded to them that "I have always considered that choosing a companion for life was a very important affair and that my happiness or misery in this life depended on the choice and for that reason I never felt myself bound to be dictated in the affair by any higher authority than my own feelings." Cornell maintained a skeptical view of religious establishments throughout his life, although he later encouraged the foundation of, and occasionally attended services at, the Unitarian Church in Ithaca.

The Cornells' marriage endured; in 1844, Ezra wrote to Mary Ann that their love had "been tried and become fixed and abiding. It is as intense as pure and as reciprocal this day after more than thirteen years trial as it was on the happy day of our union." The young couple lived in a small house they called "The Nook," and after falling out with Jeremiah Beebe, Cornell farmed there, unsuccessfully. Two of his first three children died, and were buried in the Nook's backyard, now part of Lakeview Cemetery and the site of the Cornell family's mausoleum.

Mary Ann's brother, Otis Wood, characterized Ezra as an outsider, with a "peculiarity in his early life in the way of entire forgetfulness of his own needs and those of his family." Yet

Cornell, seen by relatives as "unreasonably generous" to the public, seems to have considered money less as a means to itself than as a by-product of an ethical lifestyle, and he trusted to the righteousness of his actions to provide for his family.

Cornell held other people to high standards as well. As his brother-in-law tells it, on his original trek to Ithaca from DeRuyters, Ezra had stopped for the night along the way at a hotel, and performed what Otis characterized as "one of his Quaker capers":

> He said to the landlord, "If a decent young man were to come along and say that he had had no breakfast and had no money to buy one, what would you do?" "I would tell him come in and have something to eat," the man told him. "Well," said Mr. Cornell, "here's your chance." When he came out after he had had his breakfast, he put down twenty-five cents. "I thought you didn't have any money," says the landlord. "No, I didn't say so. I just wanted to know what you would do if I didn't have any."

The boom years of the 1830's, spurred by land and timber speculation, led Ezra to write to his father in 1834 that he "had got out of debt and a little to spare, but not being able to injoy [sic] sound sleep while I remained in that situation (a situation that some would call happy) I have removed the evil by running in debt for the large house and lot." In the bust that followed, Ezra turned to various entrepreneurial ventures including an invention of his neighbor's, the "Barnaby & Moore's Double Mold-Board Plow" which could be adjusted for the slope of the field, and bought the rights to sell the plow in Georgia and Maine.

Otis Wood called it "one of his 'bad guesses.' Georgia was coming forward at that time as the great agricultural state of the South, but when he got there he found that the plow of the state was a darkey and a hoe." Slave labor was cheaper than his modern machinery, and Cornell met with little success and many hardships on his travels. He witnessed a slave auction and was horrified by the experience. In a letter to Mary Ann he said of the South, "I don't know as it can be different where people are bred as stock and sold in the market as cattle. It is one of the evils of the cursed institution that hangs like a plague spot over a portion of America." He described the bleak conditions of his journey to his wife, calling the second-class train car "a pig pen upon wheels, or a hyena cage, with rough naked boards for seats and slides for windows…I have had to pinch clost [sic]. I am here [in North Carolina] and have got 57 cents left…I shall have to let you pay the postage on letters until I can rase [sic] the wind." Two more of their children died during his prolonged absences.

Ezra's subsequent sales trip to Maine lasted for several years. In the meantime, Mary Anne and the surviving five children got by with little at home. According to Otis, his and Mary Anne's father, a well-to-do farmer, "used to come to town with his lumber wagon loaded with things to carry the family along. And it is characteristic of [Ezra] that when he came home after a two or three years' trip, instead of bringing at least a sack of flour or something practical, he brought a trunkful of gilt-edged books…it shows the bent of the man and his lack of foresight for the family; he was a visionary. He couldn't do anything on the same plan with ordinary people. He had great plans and made great out-puts, but not for himself."

While his family struggled to make ends meet, Cornell continued to pursue his business ventures. F.O.J. Smith, editor of the *Maine Farmer* and a member of Congress, who Cornell had met while marketing his plow in Maine, engaged him to construct a machine to cut furrows for laying pipes through which the telegraph lines would be run. Ezra wrote to Mary Ann on August 6, 1843 with customary caution:

> If [the machine] succeeds it is worth thousands, and my faith is strong, as it usually is in favour of projects of my own origin…You wont get excited I trust my Dear if you should see some flourishes in the "dailies" about the success

of a rum "pipe layer" don't think because "dad" is "Esquire" that we are all Esquires. Keep cool and be ready when the bad comes round, don't leap too soon.

At this point, Ezra was still mending his own clothes on the road.

Cornell concluded that condensation in the pipes and faulty insulation of the underground wires had impeded the electric current in the lines, and determined to find a better solution for running the lines. In his *Reminiscences,* Andrew Dickson White, first President of Cornell University, describes Cornell and his typically self-taught, and stubborn, insistence on doing what he believed was best. Faced with bureaucratic resistance, White wrote, Ezra wasn't afraid to take matters into his own hands:

> Having drawn all the books on electricity that he could find in the Congressional Library, he had satisfied himself that it would be far better and cheaper to string the wires through the open air on poles. This idea was for a time resisted by the men controlling the scheme. Some of them regarded such interference in a scientific matter by one whom they considered a plain working man as altogether too presuming. But one day Professor Morse [*Samuel F. B. Morse, inventor of the telegraph*] came out to decide the matter. Finding Mr. Cornell at his machine, the Professor explained

the difficulties in the case – especially the danger of shaking the confidence of Congress, and so losing the necessary appropriation, should any change in plan be adopted – and then asked Mr. Cornell if he could see any way out of the difficulty. Mr. Cornell answered that he could: whereupon Professor Morse expressed a strong wish that it might be taken. At this Mr. Cornell gave the word to his men, started up the long line of horses dragging the ponderous machine, guided it with his own hands into a great boulder lying near, and thus broke and deranged the whole machinery...

Thanks to this stratagem, the necessary time was gained without shaking the confidence of Congress, and [Cornell] at once began stringing the wires upon poles; the insulation was found far better than in the underground system, and there was no more trouble.

Cornell subsequently made fortunes for himself and other investors building telegraph systems, and the remnants of his blue glass insulators are still to be seen in central New York and across the country. A jubilant Ezra wrote to his wife in 1844 of the telegraph, echoing the European trope of man's domination over nature, "Is not space annihilated? The critter electricity has been brought down from heaven and tamed, as mild as a dove and as gentle as a lamb, yielding obedient submission to man."

The Men Who Built Sage Hall

By 1849, Cornell had built a third of the telegraph lines in America, and was also a director and shareholder in local telegraph companies. Yet in the early fifties he found himself down-and-out again, constantly borrowing more to build more telegraphs, and reduced once to buying breakfast in New York with a dime he found walking down Broadway. His health suffered during his travels; he contracted smallpox and typhus, and even shattered an arm while riding in an open rail car. By all accounts he remained stoic throughout.

Cornell's luck changed when the consolidation of small local telegraph companies in 1855 resulted in the Western Union Telegraph Company, so named at Ezra's insistence to reflect its range from coast to coast. Cornell held 150,000 shares of stock, and in 1864 his quarterly dividends were $35,000; he returned to Ithaca a wealthy entrepreneur.

Ezra bought the DeWitt Farm in 1857, the same 500 acres between Cascadilla and Fall Creeks that he had passed through on his first journey to Ithaca, and that now comprise the university's central campus. There he pursued his vision of establishing a model scientific farm, starting out by acquiring a herd of prize-winning purebred Shorthorn cattle. As time went on, his disappointment with the quality of the science available to help farmers improve the health of their herds led to an abiding interest in agriculture education.

Cornell's social stature eventually made him a political force. A life-long Republican, he attended Lincoln's inauguration. In 1861, he was elected to the New York State Assembly, and, as Chair of the Committee on Agriculture, soon went on to become President of the New York State Agricultural Society. In this capacity, he and Mary Ann visited European farms, as well as the Exposition of the World's Industry in London and the Royal Agricultural College of England.

This position also made Cornell an ex officio trustee of Ovid Agricultural College, founded in 1853 as the first agriculture school in the United States. He became convinced of the need for a technical university for the working class of New York State, one that would teach scientific methods of farming and industry. Cornell's plan was to create an institution on his farm in Ithaca to train farmers in scientific agricultural techniques. He also wanted to develop workshops, directed by Mary Ann, to train young women in practical household skills, so that all the students could provide for their own maintenance by working part-time while they spent the rest of the day at conventional studies. The legacy of this vision is the state side of Cornell University, the Agriculture, Veterinary and Human Ecology schools.

Ezra also found his calling in philanthropy at this time, and his first act was to build a public library in Ithaca in 1863, a large building with commercial space housing the post office and bank, and an 800-seat auditorium upstairs to help finance the operation of the library. Rich beyond his expectations, Cornell wanted to use his money to help the "deserving poor"; thus he limited his own children's inheritance to $100,000 each, in his view for their own good. Ezra defined his personal philosophy in a letter to his son Alonzo in 1840: "There is no other safe rule than to establish character upon a fixed principle; do right because it is right, for the sake of the right and nothing else. Every act should be measured by that rule – 'is it right'? Let a pure heart prompt an honest conscience to answer the question and all will be well." Writing again to Alonzo in 1846, Ezra underlined his belief in the power of knowledge: "You had better pay very close attention to Mathematiks, Algebra, Geometry, Trigonometry, Civil engineering & &, with that you want to learn thoroughly the English language, History, Composition, Writing, Geography, Phylosophy, Chemistry & & [sic]." Never did a Renaissance man have higher ambitions for his progeny than those of the self-taught Ezra Cornell.

A letter to Mary Ann, in 1854, states his religious convictions, and his view of the problematic nature of organized religion, as well as his hope for the triumph of secular humanism:

The happiness of man is the completion and perfection of His works. Anything short of the full and complete happiness of man would mar the grand design of the architect of the heavens...But the gospel as it is preached...falls more like a mildew upon a benighted world, and tries to shield the deformities of the dead and putrid carcass of 'the Church' from the penetrating eye of advancing science and enlightened humanity...The steam engine, the railroad and the telegraph are the great engines of reformation, and by the time we enter upon the 20th century the present will be looked back to as we now look back to the dark ages...A new era in religion and humanity will have arrived.

The new religion of science did indeed arrive, although the humane society that Cornell predicted has proven more elusive; still, 19th century utopianism was the basis of the secular institution that he envisioned.

Andrew Dickson White's path to an educational philosophy was very different from Ezra Cornell's. Born to privilege in Homer, near Cortland, New York, he was the grandson of a rich member of the State Legislature and the son of a banker. As a child White suffered from ill health, but he was intellectually gifted and studied at home with tutors, benefiting from his father's substantial library. Andrew's parents were abolitionists, and he shared their belief that slavery had an evil effect on the society that embraced it.

The Whites were devout Episcopalians, but Andrew refused at the age of twelve to be confirmed, or to recite certain parts of the Creed. Like Ezra Cornell, he never joined a sect, ascribing instead to the enlightened liberalism of his time, and a general belief in the history of mankind as a linear progression from savagery to civilization, guided by a benevolent Creator. Science was man's (and woman's) partner in manifesting the perfect civilization that the optimistic nineteenth century America deemed possible. This philosophy, arrived at as a child, remained a lifelong theme in A.D. White's work; he would eventually publish a book, *A History of the Warfare of Science with Theology in Christendom* (1896), that reflected the struggle that Cornell University had faced as the result of its religious skepticism.

White's father initially denied A.D.'s boyhood dream of attending Harvard or Yale, insisting that he attend the Episcopal institution at Geneva that would become Hobart and William Smith Colleges. The 16 year old entered in 1849 as a sophomore, and had a dismal year. In his *Autobiography*, he wrote that he had been affiliated "as student, professor, or lecturer, with some half-dozen large universities at home and abroad, and in all of these together have not seen so much carousing and wild dissipation as I then saw in the little 'Church College' of which the especial boast was that, owing to the small number of its students, it was 'able to exercise a direct Christian influence upon every young man committed to its care.' It was my privilege to behold...even the president himself, on one occasion, obliged to leave his lecture-room by a ladder from a window, and, on another occasion, kept at bay by a shower of beer-bottles."

Andrew spent most of the year in the library, where a book about the architecture and campuses of English universities made "every feature of the little American college [seem] all the more sordid. But gradually I began consoling myself by building air-castles. These took the form of structures suited to a great university..." These daydreams were the inspiration for the future buildings of Cornell University, especially the earliest Second Empire structures on the Arts Quadrangle. A.D. White consistently pressed for the solid stone architecture, borrowed from Old World institutions, that defines the central campus today.

In a somewhat devious maneuver, young Andrew took charge of his own destiny the next fall. Ostensibly bowing to his father's demand that he return to Geneva, he actually went to the home of a former tutor and took up studies for the Yale University entrance exam. In January of 1851, his father apparently had no choice but to take him to New Haven, where he tried unsuccessfully to bribe Andrew, with the promise of a great private library, to go to Trinity instead of Yale.

A.D. White did well at Yale, but found the educational system disappointing: "There was too much reciting by rote and too little real intercourse between teacher and taught. The instructor sat in a box, heard students' translations without indicating anything better, and their answers to questions with very few suggestions or remarks...there was not, during my whole course at Yale, a lecture upon any period, subject, or person in literature, ancient or modern." Elsewhere he described the state of higher education in the mid-nineteenth century as being "as stagnant as a Spanish convent, and as self-satisfied as a Bourbon duchy." In graduate school in Germany, White became convinced that its seminar system was far superior to the English recitation system, and eventually based the Cornell humanities program on the German educational philosophy of free speculation and abstract thought.

Returning to the U.S. after years spent touring, studying and collecting books in Europe, A.D. White was offered a professorship in history at the University of Michigan in 1857. The university was founded in 1817 in Detroit about 20 years before the Michigan Territory officially became a state, and moved to Ann

The Men Who Built Sage Hall

Arbor in 1837. It was the largest of the mid-western free-minded, non-sectarian institutions of learning that had been established in the 19th century, including a few that admitted women. Oberlin College in Ohio has admitted women since 1837 (and African-Americans since its founding in 1835), and Antioch College since 1853. The University of Michigan followed suit in 1870, and by 1890 women made up a quarter of their student body.

White flourished at the University of Michigan as a popular lecturer and mentor, and even led efforts to plant avenues of elm and evergreen trees on the campus in an attempt to overcome the barrenness of the fledgling institution's quadrangle. Yet he clung to his dream of establishing a great American university in upstate New York. White's father died in 1860, leaving him a wealthy man, and he took a leave of absence from Michigan to settle the estate. In September of 1862, he wrote a proposal to Gerrit Smith, a wealthy reformer and fellow abolitionist who lived near Syracuse, asking for Smith's help in establishing a university, and pledging his entire fortune to the project. White outlined his vision, that would eventually be realized in Ithaca:

> There is needed a truly great university.
>
> First, to secure a place where the most highly prized instruction may be afforded to *all* – regardless of sex or color…

The Men Who Built Sage Hall

Fourthly, to afford an asylum for Science – where truth shall be sought for truth's sake, where it shall not be the main purpose of the Faculty to stretch or cut science exactly to fit "Revealed Religion"…

But sir, an institution to do these things must be splendidly endowed. It must have the best of Libraries – collections in the different departments – Laboratory – Observatory – Botanical Garden perhaps – Professorships – Lectureships.

If the institution is to be effective in reform it must be on such a scale as to *force* the public to respect it – and it must present such decidedly superior attractions that students will flock to it – despite the pulpits.

To admit women and colored persons into a *petty* college would do good to the individuals concerned; but to admit them to a great university would be a blessing to the whole colored race and the whole female sex – for the weaker colleges would be finally compelled to adopt the system.

White closed with an allusion to the ongoing Civil War. September of 1862 had seen the battles at Harper's Ferry, where the abolitionist John Brown was hanged after his unsuccessful attempt to attack an Army ammunitions depot, and then Antietam, the deadliest battle of the war with 5,000 dead and 20,000 wounded: "I write in one of the darkest periods of our national history; but I remember that the great University of Leyden was founded when Holland was lying in ruins. In the hope of living to see a true and liberal University in Western New York State – acting with power on a regenerate nation I am, Sir, – with great respect, Heartily yours, And. D. White." White remained faithful to his generation's belief that they were mandated to reform and even perfect western civilization.

The Morrill Land Grant College Act, signed by President Lincoln in 1862, was entitled "An act donating public lands to the several States and Territories which may provide colleges for the benefit of agriculture and the mechanic arts." Controversial because it gave federal scrips for the purchase of western lands by private investors in the land-poor eastern states, it was a perfect vehicle to enable Ezra Cornell to endow a major technical institution. In addition, now-Senator Cornell had the clout in Albany to overcome the opposition of several smaller colleges that felt equally entitled to a piece of the federal pie. Cornell tried to obtain the proceeds of the sale of New York's scrips for roughly 100,000 acres, about one tenth of the land grant, for the State Agricultural College at Ovid. However, political maneuvering by other interests resulted in a push for giving the funding to the People's College in Montour Falls, another technical school, under certain conditions requiring provision of facilities. Ultimately a bill was introduced into the Senate in January of 1864, proposing to divide the funding between the two colleges in Ovid and Montour Falls.

Labor unions from New York City were promoting the idea of an agriculture and mechanical institution in central New York. Horace Greeley was among the proponents of free public education, and a trustee of the People's College when its charter was granted by the Legislature in 1853. In 1851, Greeley wrote to Harrison Howard, founder of the College, that what he hoped for was "a People's University, wherein each student may learn whatever he needs to know with these inflexible conditions: 1. That he shall devote at least a specified portion of each day to bona fide manual labor; 2. That he shall steadily qualify himself for the efficient prosecution of some productive avocation. Of course I think it should be Farming as well as Mechanical with a Female as well as a Male Department." The College operated from 1858 to 1866, but the state funds eventually went to Ezra Cornell. Greeley became a trustee of Cornell University when it was chartered in 1865, and continued to promote equal education for women. He would write to Howard in 1871 saying, "I wish you would refer to the old People's College and say how far its aims are fulfilled in Cornell."

The Men Who Built Sage Hall

White recalls meeting Cornell in Albany around 1860:

Though his chair was near mine, there was at first little intercourse between us, and there seemed small chance of more. He was steadily occupied, and seemed to care little for making new acquaintances. He was, perhaps, the oldest man in the Senate; I, the youngest; he was a man of business; I was fresh from a University professorship; and, upon the announcement of committees, our paths seemed separated entirely, for he was made chairman of the committee on Agriculture, while to me fell the chairmanship of the committee on Education.

And yet it was this last difference which drew us together; for among the first things referred to my committee was a bill to incorporate a public library which he proposed to found in Ithaca...Ezra himself served as the project manager for the builder, scrutinizing every aspect of the construction, as he would continue to do at the future university.

On reading this bill I was struck, not merely by its provision for a gift of one hundred thousand dollars to his townsmen, but even more by a certain breadth and largeness in his way of making it. The most striking sign of this was his mode of forming a board of trustees; for, instead of the usual effort to tie up the organization forever in some sect, party, or clique, he had named the best men of his town – his political opponents as well as his friends; and had added to them the pastors of all the principle churches, Catholic and Protestant.

The Board of Trustees of the library was in fact a prototype for the diversity of the future University's Board, in that it included Cornell (and after his death his eldest male heir), clergy from all denominations in the city, principals of the schools, and citizens of the town.

A.D. White's vision of an American university was different from Ezra Cornell's, but they were complementary. White describes the situation in his *Reminiscences*: "For some years...I had been dreaming of a University, had looked into the questions involved, at home and abroad, had approached sundry wealthy and influential men on the subject, but had obtained no encouragement, until this strange and unexpected combination of circumstances – a great land grant, the use of which was to be determined largely by the committee of which I was chairman, and this noble pledge of Mr. Cornell." White worked to convince Cornell of the need for education in the humanities that included, in addition to the sciences, modern as well as ancient languages, and literature and history, a radical approach to a university curriculum at the time.

The Men Who Built Sage Hall

Ezra Cornell came to see his technical institution as part of a larger vision. The happy collaboration of the founders was that Cornell's property and fortune made possible the utilization of the Morrill Land Grant funding, while A.D. White's library made Cornell University the world-class institution it is today. In addition, both Cornell and White were firmly united against the association of any religious sect with the university; mirroring the still young nation's constitution, separation of church and school were to be complete. Non-sectarian religious services inevitably formed part of the ceremony surrounding life in 19th century society, including life at Cornell University, yet the formal separation, and lack of affiliation, was unique.

Together, White and Cornell conceived of the university that would sprout on Ezra's farm. The curriculum would combine modern and classical languages with theoretical and applied sciences, and be offered to people regardless of religious affiliation, sex or race, an iconoclastic educational philosophy that still guides the institution that calls itself the first truly American university.

White recalled that "Cornell uttered, during one of our conversations, words which showed that he comprehended the true theory of a university, words now engraved upon the Cornell University seal: 'I would found an institution where any person can find instruction in any study.'" The Cornell historian Morris

Bishop suggests that White himself, in his Plan of Organization delivered to the Board of Trustees in 1866, noted that they must remember the declaration of the founder that he "wishes to make such provision that every person can find opportunity here to pursue any study he desires." Thus, according to Bishop, "the lapidary form is that of Andrew D. White. George S. Batchellor, an intimate, testified: 'His pen traced the present motto as the language of Ezra Cornell.' White liked to improve, for publication, the utterances of his rude companions. Possibly Cornell actually said something like: 'I'd like to start a school where anybody can study anything he's a mind to.'" In any event, White introduced a bill to the New York State Senate in 1865, seeking to establish Cornell University as an institution for "the cultivation of the arts and sciences and of literature, and the instruction in agriculture, the mechanic arts and military tactics, and in all knowledge."

Cornell proposed that, in addition to buying the land scrips for 500,000 acres to endow the university, he also would give $500,000 and his farm to the cause. Intense controversy ensued in the State Assembly. At a hearing that pitted lawyers for and against dividing the funding, the proponents for division, according to A.D. White's account, "indulged in eloquent tirades against the Cornell bill as a 'monopoly,' – 'a wild project,' – 'a selfish scheme' – 'a job,' – 'a grab' – and the like; denounced Mr. Cornell roundly as 'seeking to erect a monument to himself'; hinted that he was 'planning to rob the State'; and, before he had finished, had pictured Mr. Cornell as a swindler and the rest of us as dupes or knaves…When the invective was especially bitter, he turned to me and said, 'I am not sure but that it would be a good thing for me to give the half a million to old Harvard College in Massachusetts, to educate the descendants of the men who hanged my forefathers.'"

In 1865, having suffered attacks on his character because of the profits he had realized in his land purchases under the Morrill Act that endowed the University, Cornell argued that his fortune was not only a product of his own labor, but also was "placed at the disposal of the industrial classes…My ruling passion is to dispose of so much of my property as is not required for the reasonable wants of my family in a manner that shall do the greatest good to the greatest number of the industrial classes of my native state." Eventually Cornell and White prevailed, and in 1865 in Albany, Governor Fenton signed a bill entitled "An act to establish the Cornell University."

Coeducation of women beside men had been inherent in the original plan for the university. Cornell was not only raised in the Quaker tradition of equality for women, he also recognized his own wife's contributions to his enterprises, writing to Mary Ann that he "freely acknowledge[d] that without [her] assistance at home I could never have accomplished the successes which have culminated in the university." Mary Ann had managed the farm and their scarce financial resources while Ezra was away from home, and he later credited her with full partnership in their relationship, citing her as an example of the kind of woman who deserved to receive an education at the university. Mary Ann was also a partner in Cornell philanthropy, later supporting the purchase and restoration of George Washington's Mt. Vernon in Virginia, the first publicly funded preservation project in the nation.

Cornell also recognized that one source of his wife's trials was her inability to earn money during his long absences. Although not an advocate of women's suffrage or perhaps feminism *per se*, he was pragmatic, and believed that Cornell University's mission was to provide a practical education and a means of self-support to the growing middle class of men and women.

A.D.'s mother, Clara Dickson White, was educated at the Cortland Academy, a coeducational institution. A strong influence on her son, she recalled that there, "the young men and women learned to respect each other, not merely for physical but intellectual and moral qualities; so there came a healthy emulation in study, the men becoming more manly and the women more womanly." White's concerns regarding coeducation at Cornell stemmed not from philosophical reasons but from the lack of facilities for women students at the fledgling campus.

While Ezra Cornell and Andrew White supported coeducation for women, Henry Sage actually provided the means that made Sage College a reality. His fortune, like Cornell's, was earned through his own success as an entrepreneur. Sage made his money in lumber: trees were plentiful, and water transportation was convenient for the lumber business that flourished in 19th century central New York. The massive population expansion, in the region and beyond, fed the demand for housing materials. Sage, like Cornell a largely self-educated man, became a major financial contributor to Cornell University.

Henry Sage's own life experience taught him that women needed an education in order to maintain themselves and their families in an uncertain world. His father, Charles, had followed his brothers-in-law to Ithaca from Connecticut, hoping to benefit from the economic advantages they had found as a result of the new Erie Canal system. Instead, he became increasingly unable to support his family, of which Henry was the only boy. Always the poor relation, Henry didn't get a job in his uncles' business until he was eighteen.

A few years later, his father launched another unsuccessful venture, to settle colonists in Texas. Henry wrote in his diary, "He lacks prudence – and financial wisdom. He builds baseless fabrics and centers all his hopes on them – they fail – and he builds others…but, learning nothing from experience – they meet the same fate – they contain the elements of decay – and cannot stand." The failures of the father denied the son his hope of attending Yale University; instead the young man was forced to sustain the rest of the family in their impoverished circumstances.

Henry's diary recounts a dream from this time. His father's "bitter, sarcastic smile" is turned on him in malice, pity, contempt and revenge, the dream ending in father and son murdering each other. The diary ends before we get the unfortunate boy's response to the news, a few years later, that his father had been killed by Indians on a return trip from Texas, after his ship wrecked off the coast of Florida. The sole supporter of his mother and three sisters, Sage knew the need for women to earn their own income (and the tragic loss of men during the Civil War would have made that even more obvious). Yet the social taboo of women working outside the home lingered in the society as a whole, typically limiting their choices to domestic work, or for educated women, teaching.

Like Ezra Cornell, Henry Sage believed that industry was a virtue, and that God rewarded those who did good works; but Sage's religion was evangelical, promoting self-improvement as salvation. Sage established his lumber business with John

The Men Who Built Sage Hall

McGraw (father of Jenny McGraw Fiske, and also a benefactor of Cornell University), and after making his fortune, moved to Brooklyn in 1857. He became involved in the reform movements advocated by Henry Ward Beecher, whose church he attended. Beecher's sister Catherine was a proponent of women's education, although not of suffrage for women. She believed that a suitably educated woman's place was in the home, and wrote that coeducation would be like "bringing gunpowder and burning coals into close vicinity." Ezra Cornell, having heard her speak in Ithaca in 1868, commented that "she has ideas on reforming her sex, but they are of the half bushel order." Henry Sage's vision for women's education was close to Catherine Beecher's, and her views on the importance of sunlight, fresh air and exercise for women's health influenced the floor plan of the Sage Residential College for Women, Sage's greatest legacy to the university.

Yet Sage also believed in education as a means of social improvement, and had an early interest in planning for the "people's college," becoming a financial consultant to the project. He attended the inaugural ceremonies for the university in October of 1868, held in the Cornell Library. Ezra Cornell and A.D. White were both so sick that they had to be carried to the event. Cornell spoke first, apologizing for the unfinished state of the campus, but insisting on his educational philosophy:

The Men Who Built Sage Hall

I hope we have laid the foundation of an institution which shall combine practical with liberal education, which shall fit the youth of our country for the professions, the farms, the mines, the manufactories, for the investigation of science, and for mastering all the practical questions of life with success and honor.

I believe that we have made the beginning of an institution which will prove highly beneficial to the poor young men and the poor young women of our country. This is one thing which we have not finished, but in the course of time we hope to reach such a state of perfection as will enable any one by honest efforts and earnest labor to secure a thorough, practical, scientific or classical education. The individual is better, society is better, and the state is better, for the culture of the citizen; therefore we desire to extend the means for the culture of all.

A.D. White spoke at length, emphasizing the "permeating or crowning ideas" that had guided the work of the founders:

They are two. First, the need of labor and sacrifice in developing the individual man, in all his nature, in all his powers, as a being intellectual, moral and religious…Training in history and literature comes in with training in science and the arts. There need be no cant against classical studies or for them. Their great worth for many minds cannot be denied. The most perfect languages the world has ever known will always have students. The simple principle will be that of universal liberty of choice among students.

The second of these permeating ideas is that of bringing the powers of the man, thus developed, to bear upon society…The educated men of a republic should keep control of the forum. Universities suited to this land and time should fit them to do it.

White's and Cornell's faith was in the individual, and the individual's mandate to create a more perfect world. While they did not unduly stress the secular nature of the institution they were founding, White's notes on his program demonstrate how controversial an idea that was in their day: the Governor of New York, Reuben Fenton, had come to Ithaca to take part in the ceremony, but, according to White, "was afraid of Methodists & Baptists & other sectarian enemies of the University & levanted the night before leaving the duty to Lt. Gov. Woodford who discharged the duties admirably." Politicians were held accountable to the religious establishments then, as they are in our own time.

The Men Who Built Sage Hall

Society as a whole in the 19th century was barely ready to accept a non-religious institution. As late as 1872, two years before his death, Ezra Cornell responded to a letter he had received from his distant relative William Cornell, a Presbyterian minister, who had seen the plans for Cornell University. Ezra told him, "I believe you are the first Presbyterian minister who has not consigned us to purgatory for our infidelity. I should be glad to know if you can show a 'clean bill of health' from the church authorities, or perchance you may be sliding down the same declivity to perdition that we are. I should be sorry to see the whole family of Cornells on the broad road to ruin. I had hoped at least we might clutch your skirts for salvation." Cornell's sense of humor seems intact, and even this close to death, he was clearly unrepentant for his life-long views on the religious establishment. His mysterious letter to the "Coming man and woman," placed in the Sage Hall cornerstone when it was laid, and found as a result of the renovation in 1997, would reveal Cornell's greatest fear for his beloved institution.

Ezra Cornell and A.D. White hoped to educate women at Cornell University, but without Henry Sage's emotional response to their words at the founding of the university, women may have had to wait a long time to attend Cornell. Sage's business partner John McGraw told A.D. White after the inauguration ceremonies that Sage had said to him with tears in his eyes, "John, we are scoundrels to stand doing nothing while those men are killing themselves to establish this university." Sage himself told White, "I believe you are right in regard to admitting women…When you are ready to move in this matter, let me know." Sage's philanthropy to the university resulted in not just Sage Hall and Sage Chapel, but also a book fund endowment, a school of philosophy, and an archaeological museum. Sage succeeded Ezra Cornell as Chairman of the Board of Trustees, and his family continued his commitment and generosity to the university.

Sage shared Cornell and White's world-view of the linear progression of history, and the perfectibility of human society; he read widely on phrenology, the belief popular in the 19th century that natural law was derived from the relationships among natural phenomena, notably the characteristics of an individual's cranium. He wrote in his diary in 1836 that "our happiness on earth is chiefly dependent on our own acts – on our obedience to the natural laws of the different elements of our being. When these are fully understood, their influence will be beyond calculation. We can then look for the entire supremacy of our moral and intellectual natures and it requires no stretch of the imagination to see a path opened for our eternal progression…We are acting upon the combined expression of the whole world, and the development of religion, of the principles of government, of industry in all its branches, literature, the arts and sciences – all are tending to exalt the nature of man...and ultimately to produce the highest degree of human perfection."

Sage's ideal of manhood was based on the self-made man, and in this his beliefs paralleled Ezra Cornell's; it was the quintessential American founding myth. To a reformed drinker he had employed, Henry wrote, "Full forgiveness is promised by God to all who repent and forsake their sins – Claim this promise as your right from him – and none the less from man – In doing this avoid undue depression or arrogance – but modestly and warmly claim your right to manhood as long as your life is manly."

This concept of manliness implies an ideal of womanliness as well, one that supports the patriarchal status quo as the natural order of things, and proscribes women to a subordinate role in society. Although she had attended the Albany Female Academy, Sage's wife, Susan, preferred a traditional gender role. When she learned that he would endow a women's residential hall at the university, she told him that, "you have meant to do women a great good, but you have ignorantly done them an incalculable injury." More conventionally religious than Cornell and White, Sage, in the years following the founders' deaths, would have a significant influence on the university culture, especially the lifestyle of its coeds.

But experiments in educating women, like glaciers, have a long history of advances and retreats. In the Finger Lakes region, one can arguably trace the development of the feminist movement that provided the impetus for coeducation at Cornell University back to the original inhabitants of the area.

View of Sage College from the Southwest

Courtesy of the Division of Rare and Manuscript Collections,

Cornell University Library

Chapter 2: The Woman Question

A thousand years ago, the Finger Lakes region became home to the people who call themselves the Haudenosaunee, or the "League of Peace and Power." They are also known as the "people of the long house," for their bark-covered pole lodges, and lived in the southern Appalachian Mountains before relocating to what is now central New York State.

In the Haudenosaunee creation story, God loved the area so much that he left his handprint on the land, forming the Finger Lakes. Of course it was actually the last ice age that shaped the region, as glaciers advanced and retreated five times, gouging out the north-flowing river valleys to create the lakes. The gorges were formed at that time as well, when feeder creeks carved through the glacial till, leaving 150 waterfalls within ten miles of Ithaca.

Salt deposits left by the Silurian sea that covered the area 440 million years ago (still being mined today) provided an important resource for all its inhabitants, including megafauna like the mammoths and mastodons that roamed the land together until their extinction around 10,000 years ago. When the first people settled here, they marveled at the huge bones and teeth that they found in ponds and river beds, and created legends about the giants who had been destroyed by the Great Being in a flood, similar to Old World legends about the "giants in those days," before Noah's

The Woman Question

flood. The Devonian fossil shells the people found in the shale were mysterious as well, and were valued as powerful talismans.

The Haudenosaunee cultivated maize, squash and beans, crops considered to be special gifts from the Great Spirit and protected by the Three Sisters, the spirits of the plants collectively called the De-o-ha-ko, "our sustainers" or "those who support us." The women of the tribe planted and tended these companion crops by hand with relative success in the rocky soil. Their ancient techniques preserved the topsoil, unlike the plows of Europe, and their crop yields were larger than those from the depleted fields that the Europeans left behind when they first came to the Finger Lakes area two hundred years ago.

The Cayuga and Seneca tribes built settlements along their eponymous lakes, each almost forty miles long and 400-600 feet deep, and tended orchards, vineyards and grain fields (the temperate climate created by the lakes has made the region an emerging center of viniculture since the 1960's). In Ithaca, the Cayuga tribe's main settlement was near Buttermilk Falls, at the intersection of the inlet from the lake and the falls, and was called Coreorgonel, "place of the peace pipe"; but many smaller settlements existed, and archeological traces of the original inhabitants abound in the area.

The first documented Europeans to settle in North America

The Woman Question

were French, and unlike the English, who would clear cut the forests to create farmland, the French were more likely to integrate themselves into the native economy. They learned the culture and transportation methods of the Native people, for purposes of trade and missionary work, and sometimes took indigenous wives.

Joseph-François Lafitau was one of the first French missionaries in New France. He was posted to the Jesuit Mission at Sault-Saint-Louis, established in 1676 on the southern bank of the St. Lawrence opposite Montreal, from 1712 to 1717. Lafitau was known in scientific circles for his discovery of ginseng in North America, a root whose medicinal properties had been revealed to Jesuits in China and India, and that was also used by the Haudenosaunee. By the 18th century the mission was in decline, but remained a repository of the Jesuits' fifty years of observations of the people who the French called the Iroquois.

Upon his return to France in 1724, Lafitau wrote about the customs of those people. The proto-anthropologist noted that their society was age-graded, hence controlled by the elders, and that they were matrilineal, so that in the women of the tribe,

> resides all the real authority: the lands, the fields and all the harvest belong to them; they are the soul of the councils, the arbiters of peace and war; they hold the taxes and the public treasure;

The Woman Question

it is to them that the slaves are entrusted; they arrange marriages; the children are under their authority; and the order of succession is founded in their blood.

The women's strong social position reflected their status in a subsistence economy, since women controlled the means, the products, the materials and the space of agriculture. Yet the Haudenosaunee women elders elected men as their sachems, or leaders. The interconnectedness of their social order stood in stark contrast to the stratified culture of the newcomers from Europe.

Several hundred years before Europeans came to North American, the five tribes that make up the league (the Seneca, Onondaga, Oneida, Cayuga and Mohawk) had created an agreement that allied them together against the other tribes in the region. At the height of their power, their raiding parties controlled territory from the Chesapeake Bay to the Mississippi River, and from Lake Michigan to southern Quebec, although they generally lived in their home territory of the Finger Lakes.

It has been argued that the structure of the League of Peace and Power inspired Benjamin Franklin when he drafted the Articles of Confederation. He was at least aware of the League, having written to James Parker in 1750 that, "It would be a very strange thing, if six Nations of ignorant Savages should be capable

The Woman Question

of forming a Scheme for such an Union...and yet that a like Union should be impracticable for ten or a Dozen English Colonies." Contemporary models for confederation existed in the Netherlands and Switzerland in Franklin's time, and the League's council was largely a peacekeeping rather than a governing body. Still, the Haudenosaunee women's prominence and authority in their own culture may have provided some inspiration for utopians focusing on women's rights in the relative social fluidity and multicultural reality of 19th century America.

The Haudenosaunee's territory began to shrink with the arrival of the French traders, and the tribes suffered in the 17th century from skirmishes with the French and their allies, the Algonquins. The League's crucial mistake was to side with the British, the "great white Father," who had provided them with weapons and other aid during the colonial era. In return, they not only fought for the British against the Revolutionary Army, but also supplied them with food from their granaries. In retribution, General John Sullivan, under direct orders from President George Washington, led a brutal campaign against the League, burning villages, crops and warehouses up and down the shores of the Finger Lakes in the fall of 1779.

Mary Jemison, known as the "white woman of the Genessee," was born on her family's ocean passage from Londonderry, Northern Ireland. She was 15 when her family was

The Woman Question

captured by a Shawnee and French raiding party in Pennsylvania in 1758. After her family was killed, Mary was sold to a Seneca family who adopted her into the tribe. She lived with them near Canandaigua, NY, married twice, and became an influential person in the region. Mary told her story to James E. Seaver when she was 80 years old, and the resulting *Narrative of the Life of Mrs. Mary Jemison* is a fascinating read, full of details of the Seneca lifestyle.

Mary recounted the Sullivan campaign. The tribe's scouts watched the army as it approached them, and the women and children hid in the woods. The men skirmished with the Revolutionary Army, but outnumbered, they eventually saved themselves and hid with the rest of the tribe. When it was deemed safe, all returned to the village to find that the army had "destroyed every article of the food kind that they could lay their hands on. A part of our corn they burnt, and threw the remainder into the river. They burnt our houses, killed what few cattle and horses they could find, destroyed our fruit trees, and left nothing but the bare soil and timber." Realizing that there would be no food for her four children, Mary led them away through the forest, finding shelter with "two negroes, who had run away from their masters sometime before." She worked for them that winter, and subsequently bought land in the area.

The Woman Question

In General Sullivan's letter to Congress of 1779, he describes his army's enthusiasm, despite their low provisions, to raze the area: "I was...encouraged in the belief, that I should be enabled to effect the destruction and total ruin of the Indian territories by this truly noble resolution of the army." He reported their progress, in the Cayuga's territory alone, as the destruction of "five principal towns and a number of scattering houses, the whole making about one hundred in number exceedingly large and well built...and also destroyed two hundred acres of excellent corn with a number of orchards, one of which had in it 1500 fruit trees...The number of towns destroyed by this army amounted to 40 besides scattering houses. The quantity of corn destroyed, at a moderate computation, must amount to 160,000 bushels, with a vast quantity of vegetables of every kind." This was true slash-and-burn warfare, designed to drive the native people from the region. The tribes were forced to flee to the west, and many people died during that exceptionally harsh winter, camped outside the British fort at Niagara Falls, but receiving little aid from the British.

When many Iroquois were placed on reservations after the American Revolution, efforts were made to "improve" them. As a result, the traditional male activities of hunting and trade were curtailed, and the adoption of European social structures transferred the dominance of mother-daughter relationships to a husband-wife relationship and a focus on the nuclear family. This and a legacy of neglect have created social problems that have plagued the tribes since their displacement, although in some areas now the unemployment and poverty are mitigated by gambling casinos that the tribes are allowed to operate as sovereign territories. The Haudenosaunee are still a strong presence in the Finger Lakes region: to this day, lawsuits on the part of the Cayuga tribe contest the ownership of their tribal lands, citing a treaty with the Federal government that predated an agreement with New York State, thus rendering the state treaty illegal. Current landowners naturally protest the First People's claim, but perhaps the Cayuga will eventually receive some of the land that is now protected as a wildlife refuge at the northern end of the lake as partial compensation.

The land around Seneca and Cayuga Lakes was divided into tracts that were awarded to American soldiers, the acreage based on their rank, who received the land as payment for their service from a government short of cash. Relatively few of them actually settled their tracts, but there were fortunes to be made from land speculation, development and sale. Simeon DeWitt, Surveyor General of New York State, bought most of what is now the City of Ithaca, everything between the hills, from his father-in-law, who had in turn bought it from soldiers. DeWitt's enlightened layout of the original town center is still evident in Ithaca's historic downtown district, with its central square surrounded by churches and a mixed-use former school built on land that he donated to the village.

The bear and deer paths that the First People traveled and improved became in turn the wagon wheel ruts followed by the steady stream of settlers from the eastern seaboard, headed west. Rivers and lakes in upstate New York were also main routes of travel and transport, but the terrain required many portages over waterfalls on the western route. Nevertheless, many settlers outfitted their covered wagons in Albany and followed the waterways west to Ohio. Politicians including Governor DeWitt Clinton, and landowners, many of them speculators who had purchased the land hoping to profit from the development of western New York, envisioned a navigable waterway that would link the east coast to Ohio, then the western frontier.

Building a canal from Albany to Lake Ontario's eastern shore would have been an easier way to open navigation to the larger world, via the St. Lawrence River, but the New Yorkers wanted to cut Canada out of the action, for economic reasons and also due to lingering hard feelings about the Revolutionary War. Thomas Jefferson and George Washington opposed their plan, hoping instead to build a canal from the Chesapeake Bay to Pittsburgh, thus benefiting the Commonwealth of Virginia, but the topography of the area did not favor that plan. Downstate New York politicians, for their part, refused to support the project, seemingly unable to grasp the profits that New York City would realize from the canal.

The construction of the Erie Canal is a metaphor for its time: the project of 19th century America was nation-building, and a few strong individuals used local resources to build what was then the largest canal in the world. They conceived of their project in no less terms, and were convinced that by opening the way to the fertile wilderness west of the Hudson River the canal would transform New York into the "Empire State." They turned out to be right.

The canal commissioners' conviction that they could achieve their goal, to open the frontier in New York from the Hudson River to Lake Erie, was joined to their faith that God had presented them with a ready-made route that they were morally (and economically) obliged to improve, for the good of the country and the state. Incredibly, a team of practically self-taught upstate surveyors and engineers, leading crews of laborers, local farm-boys or Irish immigrants, slogged through mosquito-ridden swamps and dug locks out of waterfalls, building one of the engineering marvels of its age in only five years.

Nicknamed "Clinton's Ditch," the Canal was a major conduit after 1825 for the 100,000 people each year who traveled across the state to the western frontier of Ohio, many of them immigrants from Germany or Ireland. Water powered lumber, grist and textile mills sprang up alongside the canals, contributing to the social instability of the frontier towns. Even among the earlier European settlers, social patterns changed as men and women left farming to work in the expanding industrial economy.

Both Ithaca and Syracuse owe their existence to their locations on the water system that linked them to the outside world, and both were transportation hubs, for lumber in Ithaca, and for salt and eventually wheat in Syracuse. The Erie Canal facilitated communication with the outside world in this otherwise remote region, yet the frontier society nurtured free thinkers who were relatively free to invent themselves outside the confines of the conservative East Coast.

By the mid-nineteenth century, upstate New York was a hotbed of reformers, home not only to utopian communities and independent religious sects like the Shakers and Mormons, but also to abolitionists and nascent feminists. They shared a conviction that destiny favored their young nation, and that all its citizens were part of a grand scheme to improve and expand civilization. These radicals believed that they could change the world, and the evidence surrounding them, like the Erie Canal, only fanned the fires of their belief.

The Woman Question

New York State had abolished slavery in 1827. When the Slave Recovery Act of 1850 authorized agents from slave states to hunt for freedom seekers in the free states and return them to slavery, many people in upstate New York resented the unwelcome interference of the federal government coming to take away their African American neighbors. There was strong regional support for the Underground Railroad, that moved freedom seekers north to Lake Ontario and Canada, which as a British territory had abolished slavery in 1833. From Harriet Tubman, the "Moses of her People," who risked her life many times to bring her family and others to freedom from Maryland to the Canadian border via her home in Auburn, New York, to William Henry Seward, Secretary of State to Abraham Lincoln and also a resident of Auburn, to the AME Zion Church in Ithaca, there were many stewards and stops along the Railroad in central New York in the years leading up to the Civil War.

The abolition movement set the stage for the activists who would make New York State the center for social reform movements that were integral to the educational projects of men like Ezra Cornell and A.D. White, the founders of Cornell University. Public education became a priority in the state, and common schools were established for boys and girls in the newly formed villages and towns. A shortage of teachers led to the development of "normal schools," where women as well as men were trained to teach, and women took on the role of primary school educators, a field that they still dominate.

Women became central figures in the reform movement, and were especially active in the abolitionist cause, a moral issue for many Northerners. Temperance was inherently a women's issue as well, since men were legally entitled to spend all their pay on alcohol, leaving their wives and families destitute. Two prominent women in the reform movement were from upstate New York, Susan B. Anthony and Elizabeth Cady Stanton.

Women's rights have waxed and waned in history, but the roots of what we call the women's movement predate the European presence in America, running back to the Renaissance. In France, women's rights declined as the population moved from the countryside to the city and the relatively egalitarian society of the village gave way to the fixed hierarchies of larger social structures. French noblewomen's rights were eroded through legislation passed by the newly centralized church/state: by 1464, France had passed the Salic law, preventing a woman from inheriting the French crown. Compared to the former customary social arrangements, which had made it possible for women to inherit property and businesses from their husbands and fathers, women progressively lost property and inheritance rights in the centuries that followed.

The Woman Question

Even upper-class women were systematically disenfranchised. A notable example is Christine De Pizan, a recognized poet and official biographer of Charles V of France. She played a major role in the *querelle des femmes*, the "woman question" that occupied the intellectuals of Europe in early modern times. In 1405 she wrote *The Book of the City of Ladies*, in which she catalogued courageous and astute women from ancient history, allegorically arguing that great women were equal to great men in every way. Of course, most people in early modern Europe were illiterate peasants, and rights for either sex of their station were non-existent.

As the printing press made a more literate society possible, the education of women in an upper-class (or upwardly mobile) home took place in the family library, and in England by the 18th century it was even possible for girls to receive a primary education in a private institution. Mary Woolstonecraft, the author of the seminal *Vindication of the Rights of Women* (1792), attended a day school until she was 15 (while her brother received a full formal education). Mary and her sisters were destined to be governesses, since the family had no money for dowries; instead they started their own school, teaching in accordance with Mary's child-rearing theories. She emphasized giving a child room to play and think, teaching hygiene and healthy life-styles, as well as critical thinking and a generally holistic approach to education. Mary was also an advocate of breast-feeding when only the poorest of the poor practiced that – all in all, well ahead of her time.

A marriage act of 1753 had stripped married Englishwomen of rights to their own property, children, and earnings, and even of the right to divorce. No wonder Mary Woolstonecraft wrote against the institution of marriage as she knew it. Yet she married the philosopher William Godwin when she became pregnant with his child, Mary Woolstonecraft Godwin, but died tragically after the birth of the child. Mary Godwin went on to marry the poet Shelley, and write the gothic novel *Frankenstein* (1831), about the evil effect of not nurturing the being that one creates. In fact, whatever their personal problems, these proto-feminists were entirely focused on education, and convinced that it was the key to a new world order, based on a model of domestic peace and respect.

They didn't live to see it, of course, and Woolstonecraft and her ideological sisters paid a high price for their denial of society's ways: children are turned over to fathers never to be seen again, lovers with no legal obligations move on to greener pastures, inheritances are stripped away – all within the bounds of the law. Their legacy lives on in their writings. They taught a subversion of the upper-class model of education, the recitations and useless knowledge, that in its pragmatic approach was attractive to the aspiring middle-class; but most strongly they spoke for an education for women that would transcend their own limited opportunities.

The problematic education of upper class women in nineteenth century England is central to the novel *Aurora Leigh* (1857), and its author, Elizabeth Barrett Browning, grew up reading Woolstonecraft. Considered standard reading itself until the early 20th century, especially for American women, *Aurora Leigh* has been rediscovered by a new generation of feminist readers. In it, Aurora, a writer, struggles with the male-dominated intellectual climate of her time. Her father had given her a liberal education, teaching her himself from his extensive library; but after both her parents die, the budding intellectual's instruction is circumscribed by her custodial aunt's conventional taste in "womanliness":

> I learnt my complement of classic French
> (Kept pure of Balzac and neologism)
> And German also, since she liked a range
> Of liberal education, – tongues, not books.
> I learnt a little algebra, a little
> Of the mathematics, – brushed with extreme flounce
> The circle of the sciences, because
> She misliked women who are frivolous...
> By the way,
> The works of women are symbolical.
> We sew, sew, prick our fingers, dull our sight,

The Woman Question

Producing what? A pair of slippers, sir,
To put on when you're weary – or a stool
To stumble over and vex you…'curse that stool!'
Or else at best, a cushion, where you lean
And sleep, and dream of something we are not
But would be for your sake. Alas, alas!
This hurts most, this – that, after all, we are paid
The worth of our work, perhaps.

Browning scorned the "accomplishments in girls" valued by her society, and the complicity of women in a culture that devalued them. Her frustration with educated women's work resonated with the nascent feminists in America. Susan B. Anthony always carried the copy of *Aurora Leigh* that her mother had given her on her lecturing circuit, calling it her most cherished book.

While privileged women in nineteenth century New York, as in Europe, did have access to education in family libraries and from tutors, there was still little public education for girls or women anywhere in the world. While many young women attended "finishing schools" specializing in the sort of education Browning disparaged, upstate New York was also home to some of the earliest women's colleges, including the Troy Female Seminary, founded by Emma Willard (1821), the Genesee Wesleyan Seminary (1832), and Elmira College (1855). Still, not

The Woman Question

much had changed in a century, and most of the colleges prepared women to teach in primary and secondary schools.

The passage of the Morrill Act helped to advance the cause of education for women. Coeducation did not exist on the college level until Oberlin College in Ohio allowed four women to study there in 1837, awarding three of them degrees in 1841; Antioch College was next in 1853. By 1900, 70% of U.S. colleges admitted women, leading educators to term coeducation a dead issue. Still, the prestigious eastern universities remained all-male institutions into the second half of the 20th century; Cornell was the first Ivy League school to admit women, but followed the Universities of Iowa (1856), Wisconsin (1860), Washington (1862) and Michigan (1870) in Oberlin's footsteps in 1872.

The lobbying for coeducation in New York State began well before that. Elizabeth Cady Stanton lived in Seneca Falls, just up the lake from Ithaca, and organized the first women's rights convention there in 1848. As she wrote in *The History of Woman's Suffrage*, "A full report of the women's rights agitation in the State of New York would in a measure be the history of the movement" in the world. The daughter of a judge, and married to an anti-slavery lawyer, Cady Stanton followed the logical thread from rights for blacks to rights for women. The women's rights movement was also allied with the Utopian reform religions of the frontier; the Quakers especially had historically encouraged the education of women and their equal status in the community as a morally uplifting influence on society as a whole.

Although she was educated at Willard's Seminary in Troy, Elizabeth Cady was denied admission to higher education because of her sex. Instead, she learned from her father, a judge, that the law treated women as dependents to their male relatives in property and civil matters, and she worked against that injustice her whole life. While newlyweds, Elizabeth and her husband, the abolitionist Henry Stanton, attended the World Antislavery Convention in London in 1840 as part of the New York delegation. The women of the group were initially refused entry to the hall and finally segregated on a riser in the back. Feeling slighted, Cady Stanton and Lucretia Mott, a Quaker minister from Watertown, N.Y., angrily paced the streets of London, and decided to convene a meeting concerning women's rights when they returned to the U.S.

The result was the Women's Rights Convention that they organized in Seneca Falls on the 20th of July, 1848. The convention adopted Stanton's *Declaration of Sentiments*, inspired by the Declaration of Independence. In it, she declared that:

The Woman Question

Whereas, the great precept of nature is conceded to be, "that man shall pursue his own true and substantial happiness," therefore,

Resolved, That such laws as conflict, in any way, with the true and substantial happiness of woman, are contrary to the great precept of nature, and of no validity.

A modern reader can scarcely comprehend how radical this manifesto was in 1848, also the year that women gained the right to own property in New York State. The product of an elite education herself, equal coeducation was central to Stanton's argument for enfranchising women.

Susan B. Anthony was managing her family's farm outside of Rochester, N.Y., having retired from teaching school, when she met E.C. Stanton in 1851. Constrained by her domestic responsibilities from touring, Stanton wrote most of the speeches that were delivered by Anthony, who spoke indefatigably in the region's cities, and ultimately around the country and abroad, advocating women's right to vote and to pursue an education. The two women shared a passion for reform, whether the cause was abolition of slavery, temperance, or women's rights, and the first time they worked together was to advocate a place for women in the People's College that was being discussed by the State Legislature.

The Woman Question

Anthony wrote to Stanton in 1856, begging her to write a speech advocating public education for girls equal to that of boys, to deliver to teachers' conferences throughout New York. The letter is a poignant reminder of the everyday difficulties facing the campaign for women's rights, and sets out an early formulation of Anthony's underlying philosophy. Her sense of urgency is evident, as she asks Stanton to "load her gun" (emphases hers):

> And Mrs Stanton, <u>not</u> a <u>word</u> <u>written</u> on that Address for Teachers Conference –<u>This</u> week was to be <u>leisure</u> to me – & lo, our <u>girl</u>, <u>a wife</u>, had a miscarriage on Tuesday, – at eve one Lady Visitor came & today a man & the mercy only knows when I can get a moment – & what is <u>worse</u>, as the <u>Lord knows full well</u>, is, that if I <u>get</u> <u>all the time</u> the <u>world has</u> – <u>I can't get up a decent document</u>, so for the love of me, & for the saving of the <u>reputation</u> of <u>womanhood</u>, I beg you with one baby on your knee & another at your feet & four boys whistling buzzing hallooing Ma Ma set your self about the work – it is but small moment <u>who writes</u> the Address, but of <u>vast moment</u> that it be <u>well done</u>. I promise you to work hard, oh, how hard, & <u>pay you whatever you say</u> for your <u>time</u> & <u>brains</u> – but oh Mrs. Stanton <u>don't</u> say <u>no</u>, nor <u>don't delay</u> it a moment, for I must have it all done & <u>almost commit</u> it to memory.

The Woman Question

Stanton did write the speech, and Anthony delivered it, first at conventions of the state teachers' association, and then as the basis for a public lecture proclaiming that "to earn their bread and live is the work of both sexes. Every woman is born into the world alone and goes out of the world alone." The women's message was about equal opportunity, but also about self-fulfillment.

When Anthony gave the speech to a teacher's convention in Troy, NY, in 1856, she emphasized the point that women's education was crucial for the women's own development, regardless of the benefits that might accrue to society as a result of their education:

> In a full review of this whole subject, in reading over Educational Reports and Inaugural addresses of some of the best minds of the day, I see that man has not yet grasped the idea, that woman needs to be educated for her own individual happiness. Educate her, say they, because she is to be the mother of sons, the teacher of children, the companion of men. *All very well.* But no one seems to think of her *own pleasure* and *enjoyment*, of her *own discipline* and *development*, of the education it would bring to her own soul.

The campaign for women's rights reached its peak in the years before the Civil War, but was suspended after the start of the war, a decision that Stanton and Anthony later regretted. Neither woman lived to see their struggle for women's suffrage rewarded, and they felt the sting when their efforts contributed to the voting rights of African American men with the passage of Lincoln's Emancipation Act of 1860. Women would not get the vote until 1920.

Susan B. Anthony went so far as to cast an illegal ballot in a Rochester election in 1872, and was arrested for her act. Stanton wrote of the event with humor, questioning the contradictory, albeit traditional, bases upon which women's suffrage was denied:

> Catherine Stebbins is denied the right to vote in Michigan because she is a married woman, while Annette Gardner at the same time is allowed to vote because she is a widow. Are these men blind that they do not see they are offering bounties on sending husbands off at pack horse speed to heaven? We might think these thrusts at marriage were a premium on celibacy, but lo! Susan B. Anthony, a Republican spinster in Rochester, N.Y., having duly registered her name and voted, is arrested by U.S. Republican officers for voting a clean Republican ticket.

Anthony was convicted, but never paid the $100 fine.

E.C. Stanton was still writing over forty years after the Declaration of Rights was adopted by the Women's Rights Convention in Seneca Falls. In her famous "Solitude" speech, delivered to the Committee of the Judiciary in Washington in 1892, she lobbied for a sixteenth amendment guaranteeing the rights of women (the Equal Rights Amendment of the 1970's was passed by Congress, but not ratified by enough states to become law):

> The isolation of every human soul and the necessity of self-dependence must give each individual the right to choose his own surroundings. The strongest reason for giving woman all the opportunities for higher education, for the full development of her faculties, forces of mind and body; for giving her the most enlarged freedom of thought and action; a complete emancipation from all forms of bondage, of custom, dependence, superstition; from all the crippling influences of fear, is the solitude and personal responsibility of her own individual life.

Here the feminist cause converged with the individualistic philosophy of nineteenth century America. Still, one wonders at the energy of these reform women, and at their insistence that they be heard, in a political climate that could regard their suffragist and populist movement with such fear and loathing. Susan B. Anthony was relentlessly ridiculed for her supposedly mannish ways, frequently caricatured in male attire on broadsheets. But Anthony's motto, "Failure is impossible," reflects her times; her generation not only believed that they were on the cusp of a new and better world, but also that it was their moral obligation to do anything within their power to bring the new age to fruition.

In 1869, Susan B. Anthony came to Ithaca to deliver her speech on coeducation in "Library Hall," Ezra Cornell's first gift to the town, and declared to the crowd that "the day in which the constitution of the university should be amended so that women might be admitted to all its benefits and privileges, on the same terms as men, would be celebrated hereafter as sacredly as the Fourth of July or the day of the birth of Jesus Christ." Ezra Cornell, who had introduced her rather bluntly, saying that he "should have thought she would be independent enough to introduce herself," found her in retrospect an "ungentle advocate of the rights of the gentle sex." But he responded positively to the audience's request for his judgment that women who passed the state entrance exams would be admitted to his university.

Ezra Cornell, A.D. White, and Henry Sage all agreed that girls deserved and must receive an education that would enable them, at the very least, to attempt self-sufficiency in an unstable world without social safety nets. In this context, it's easy to see why the stage was set for the experiment of coeducation at Cornell University.

Ezra Cornell had seen the need for women to support themselves. His sister Phoebe was one of the early women telegraph operators; he gave money to the Ithaca women's war-relief organization to provide employment for soldier's wives. Two of his daughters attended Vassar, whose charter he had signed as an Assemblyman. Ezra's wife Mary Ann scooped the second shovel-full of dirt at the groundbreaking ceremony, and he credited her as much as himself for the existence of the university.

It is clear from a letter that Ezra wrote from Albany to his young granddaughter Eunice in 1867, two years before the university opened, that he intended the institution to be coeducational:

> My Dear Grand Daughter. Your little letter came duly to hand and I was very glad to hear from you, and Grand Ma was also very glad to hear from [you]. I shall be very glad when I get through with the business here so I can go home and see you and your little brothers, and have you and them go with me up on the hill to see how the workmen get along with the building of the Cornell University where I hope you and your brothers and your cousins and a great many more children will go to school when they get large enough and will learn a great many things that will be useful to them and make them wise and good women and men. I want to have girls educated in the University as well as boys, so that they may have the same opportunity to become wise and useful to society that the boys have. I want

you to keep this letter until you grow up to be a woman and want to go to a good school where you can have a good opertunity [sic] to learn, so you can show it the President and Faculty of the University to let them know that it is the wish of your Grand Pa, that girls as well as boys should be educated at the Cornell University.

The astronomer Maria Mitchell, who in 1848 became the first woman admitted to the American Academy of Sciences, was educated by her father. She became a professor at Vassar College, the first women's college considered to enforce high academic standards, and wrote to Ezra Cornell in 1868: "I consider Vassar College to be the best institution in the world *of the kind*; it is not of the right kind. When I was last in Boston I asked Dr. Hill, President of Harvard College: 'How soon will girls enter Harvard College?' and he replied: 'The most conservative member of the Faculty says: 'in twenty years.' (It's my opinion, that if you remove the zero from the number of years, you will be nearer the truth). I also asked Prof. Pierce, the Mathematics Professor: 'If a girl knocks at your classroom door and asks for admission to your class, what will you do?' He replied: 'I couldn't turn her away and I wouldn't.'" Radcliffe College formally merged with Harvard in 1977, making it a coeducational institution.

Needless to say, Prof. Mitchell urged Cornell to admit women to the university he was planning, and pointed out that other schools were also under pressure to admit women, writing that "if you <u>lead</u>, you must step quickly, for the world moves." She was intrigued by the non-sectarian nature of his university, asking "Can you keep to that?" She noted the lack of models for a secular institution, but added, "I believe that the cause of true religion is hurt every day, by those narrow lines of distinctions, on unimportant points."

Yet even Ezra Cornell could not deny the logistical problems of coeducation. He wrote to Lucy Washburn, an early applicant, that he wanted to see women educated at Cornell with their brothers, "all working smoothly and in good harmony for their best good – but I don't want them forced upon us before we are prepared to make a success of it."

A.D. White was cognizant in turn of the real opposition to admitting women to institutions of higher education, especially from the more conservative members of the State Legislature. He avoided mentioning coeducation, using the word "person" instead of man or woman, in Cornell University's charter. In this he followed the example of the University of Michigan's statute with the same language, even though Michigan's regents' committee had cited the precedent of the British legalist William Blackstone to argue that women were not persons in the eyes of the law, in order to block their admission to that university.

The Woman Question

White wrote, "I recognized obstacles to (coeducation) in the older institutions which did not exist in the newer, but I had come to believe that where no special difficulties existed, women might well be admitted to University privileges." White noted that his mother, Clara Dickson, was "one of the most conservative of women, a High-Church Episcopalian and generally averse to modern reforms; but on my talking over with her some of my plans for Cornell University, she said, 'I am not sure about your other ideas, but as to the admission of women, you are right." As a freshman, your author lived in a dormitory built at Cornell's North Campus in 1946 that bears Clara's name, which has been a coeducational facility since the 1970's.

A.D. White was approached by women's colleges interested in forming partnerships with Cornell University, including Catherine Beecher who wished to establish a women's school in Ithaca to train women in domestic science, and to prepare specially talented women for admission to the university. But White and Cornell were firm in their determination to include women in the university itself, and not an auxiliary institution, just not until they were able to accommodate them.

Not all on campus agreed, including many of the faculty. Goldwin Smith, Professor of English, was one of the most vocal opponents, having written to White in 1870 that "the speedy introduction of female students into Cornell University (meant) farewell…in that case, to all our hopes for the future generations of the institution – at least to all mine." In an editorial in the campus newsletter, *The Era,* Smith wrote that, "Apart from any objections to the particular scheme, a University so recently founded and with its reputation still to win, cannot afford to be opening its gates to every hobby…A University which in advance of public opinion offers itself as a *corpus vile* for public experiments will certainly forfeit public confidence." Smith also claimed that subjecting women to competitive examinations would be too stressful for their delicate constitutions.

Smith's objections were shared by many male students, who simply didn't want to be in classrooms with women. *The Era* voiced these feelings: "The conservative gentleman has been scandalized by the open invasion of the sacred precincts of learning. The heart of this disciple of precedent has grown heavy within him to see all the old traditions of college life, like dusty cobwebs, swept away…these fair creatures, whom he had set apart as something not to be profaned by association with prosaic toil, he finds with him in the classroom, their faces flushed with emulation, the spirit of rivalry in their eyes. To one who has associated women purely with the home-life he has enjoyed only once a year, to such a one the presence of women in college halls has all the appearance of sacrilege." Perhaps this conservative gentleman's family had (female) servants to perform the "prosaic toil" of daily life.

The thinly veiled paranoia of the male students is revealed in the satirical prediction of the future of the women in the *Cornellian* yearbook during the construction of Sage Residential College for Women in 1873: "A halo of light will emanate from Sage College, its brilliancy almost eclipsing the sun. An atmosphere of knowledge will surround this immaculate asteroid, concealing its surface from the rest of the universe. The young planet will grow in size as well as increase in population, and finally, wandering off through the heavens will leave this wretched world behind. And all this to be the result of Co-education." It's hard to imagine a more self-serving prediction than that the women's success would somehow eliminate them from the competition.

Morris Bishop writes:

The first *Cornellian*, published by the secret societies in 1869, editorialized that "The Woman's Rights monomaniacs are attempting to mislead the public into the belief that female students are to be admitted here. The foundation of the rumor probably exists only in the imagination of some enthusiasts, who, thinking that the thing ought to be so, unhesitatingly sets up the cry that it is

The Woman Question

so...We sincerely trust that Cornell University will never come to be ranked among the Oberlins of America."

It took a while for the young men to warm up to the idea of coeducation: in 1872, the senior class voted 37 against the idea, and 15 in favor; by 1876 the senior men were split evenly on the issue, 29-29.

A.D. White was not opposed to coeducation in theory, but, while it was "very difficult to see why the experiment should not succeed," he also didn't see how the fledgling institution could physically accommodate female students. Some women had tried; one of the original co-eds, Jennie Spencer, had arrived in Ithaca in 1870 from her home in Cortland. Since she was the winner of a state scholarship, White decided that he was required to admit Spencer under the state charter. He noted that "the lady student proved excellent from every point of view, and her admission made a mere temporary ripple on the surface of our affairs." Temporary indeed, since she withdrew after a few weeks. The campus housing in Cascadilla Hall was reserved exclusively for the male students, and professors and their wives. Well before trolleys would make the trip up the 400-foot hill from her rooming house downtown, Jennie would have made the onerous walk to the campus on her own.

The Woman Question

Henry Sage recognized the need for on-campus housing for women students, and pressed his case to the Board of Trustees in 1871:

> I propose to give to Cornell University for the purpose of establishing means for the better education of women, and conditioned that the said Cornell University shall provide and forever maintain facilities for the education of women as broadly as for the education of men – Two hundred and fifty thousand dollars – One hundred and fifty thousand dollars to be used for the needful buildings and equipment, and one hundred thousand dollars for endowment.

> I will advance for the construction of the buildings, as needed, and in such sums as may be required by the Trustees, seventy-five thousand dollars per year during the years 1872 and 1873, and will provide for the endowment one hundred thousand dollars in cash or approved securities, on or before the first day of August, 1874, provided the buildings are at that time completed and ready for use, and if not, within thirty days from the date of their completion.

The Board was not immediately convinced that the bequest would be in the best interest of the university, but agreed to allow a committee headed by A.D. White, and including Sage and four other board members, to be formed to research the radical idea. The men visited coeducational institutions in the Midwest, speaking with administrators, professors and students, and wrote up their findings in a lengthy report. In Albany on February 13, 1872, White read the entire document to the meeting of the Trustees, and after those mind-numbing ninety minutes, the Trustees acquiesced to Sage's offer.

In his "Report submitted to the Board of Trustees of Cornell University, in behalf of a Majority of the Committee on Mr. Sage's Proposal to Endow a College for Women," White tells the group that the committee had consulted educators with experience in coeducation, rather than with educational authorities in single sex institutions. He notes that the University of Michigan had consulted those authorities earlier, when considering the idea of coeducation at its institution, and that:

> The result is what might have been expected. It was as if the Japanese authorities aroused to the necessity of railroads and telegraphs, had corresponded with eminent Chinese philosophers regarding the ethics of the subject, instead of sending persons to observe the working of railroads and telegraphs where they are already in use...It was declared to be 'contrary to nature,' 'likely to produce confusion,' 'dangerous,' 'at variance with the ordinances of God'; in short, every argument that a mandarin would be sure to

evolve from his interior consciousness against a railroad or a telegraph which he had never seen, these correspondents reproduced against a system of education which they had never tried.

The Committee noted that young people had been attending coeducational normal schools for years, and indeed,

> with no well-watched quadrangles, no system of proctors to restrain the young men, of matrons to guard the young women…the successful education of youth of both sexes – of marriageable age – coming from distant homes, left to themselves almost entirely as to their choice of homes and associations, guided by their own judgment as to social intercourse and general conduct, is a *fact*, a fact not confined to recent experience, not restricted to a narrow territory, but a fact of many years' standing, a fact established in nearly every county of this and neighboring States.

Despite this fact, the Committee felt compelled to address the critics of coeducation. While some worried that the men would lose their "manliness," the report concluded that "men may lose their roughness and boorishness and loud self-assertion, while they increase their self-respect, manliness and true bravery… From no Colleges did a more hardy, manly, brave body of young men go into our armies than from Oberlin and Antioch. By that the charge of *effeminacy* is effectually dispelled." This refers to the Civil War, and Cornell University in turn has received many veterans' honors in the ensuing national conflicts.

The Committee rejected the idea that women would lower the standards of education at Cornell, saying that "all facts observed are in opposition to this view...[and] the young women are at least equals of the young men in collegiate studies." The Committee found that the facts also refuted the claim that women would distract the men from their studies, adding that "the desire to appear to good advantage before the young women will prove a powerful stimulus to the young men." Addressing the historical claim that rigorous mental work would jeopardize the health of young women, they point to the facts indicating that "the health of the young women is quite as good in college as out of it." This may not be surprising from an historical perspective, considering the relative lack of hygiene and the stress of childbearing in the general female population at the time.

Regarding the concern that men and women students would form romantic liaisons, the Committee rhetorically asked, "How do young men and young women form such engagements *now?*" and cautioned that,

> It is a matter of notoriety that these engagements – the most important of life, – are, as a rule, formed with less care,

foresight and mutual knowledge, than any other. Choice is determined by mere casual meeting, by an acquaintance of a few weeks, by winning manners at a ball, by a pleasing costume in the street, and at the best by a very imperfect revelation of those mental and moral qualities which are to make or mar the happiness of all concerned. Should such engagements be formed in a University where both sexes are educated together, they would be based upon a far more thorough and extended knowledge, upon an admiration of a much higher range of qualities, and upon a similarity of taste and temper, which could not be gained elsewhere.

The report points out that an education could only help to prepare women for the traditional role of helpmeet of man: "Under this [opposing] theory, as thus worked out, the aid and counsel and solace fail just when they are most needed. In their stead the man is likely to find some scraps of philosophy begun in boarding-schools, and developed in kitchens or drawing-rooms." One of their arguments was in fact the desirable cultivation of suitable wives for the isolated frontier community.

With all the goodwill that this report represents, it's also hard not to sense the committee's ambivalence towards coeducation, or to feel that these men were simply giving the idea the benefit of the doubt. The final pages of the report are especially interesting in that they seem to contradict, in part, the findings of the Committee, and in so doing to reproduce, again in part, the arguments that it had set out to refute.

For example, the report suggests that women are sensual creatures, unable to control themselves, and complains of the extravagance of poorly educated women, whose husbands then "in vast numbers, especially in our cities and large towns, are harnessed to work as otherwise they would not be; their best aspirations thwarted, their noblest ambitions sacrificed, to enable the 'partners of their joys and sorrows' to vie with each other in reproducing the last grotesque absurdity issued from the precincts of Notre Dame de Lorette, or to satisfy other caprices not less ignoble... Even the love of art they have is tainted with 'Parisian fashions'" (peculiar words from the Europhile A.D. White).

The report concludes that these weak women must be fortified against foreign temptations, and thus their education becomes a means of infusing them with "ideas which would enable woman to wield religion, morality and common sense against this burdensome perversion of her love for the beautiful." These pragmatists facilitated women's education, but their philosophy was far from Susan B. Anthony's plea that women had a right to enjoy the love of learning for itself.

Oddly, the Committee goes on to claim that women were behind the witchhunts of the Middle Ages. While there were no doubt female collaborators, modern scholars blame that phenomenon on the male-dominated institutions of the day that systematically (and cynically) persecuted poor, defenseless countrywomen, appropriating their farms in an age of shrinking land resources and burgeoning population growth. But in this Committee's telling, the "fetichisms [sic] and superstitions of this world are bolstered up mainly by women...The greatest aid which could be rendered to smooth the way for any noble thinkers who are to march through the future, would be to increase the number of women who, by an education which has caught something from manly methods, are prevented from clinging to advancing thinkers or throwing themselves hysterically across their pathway." All the usual stereotypes of women, first rejected and then represented in this report – hysteria, mental feebleness, backwardness – are a reminder that it would be another half century before women in the United States procured the right to vote.

Here again, as well, we have the dichotomy of the "womanly woman" and the "manly man," and a sense of how rigid gender divisions were in the 19th century, well before society recognized homosexual identities let alone individual sexual rights. On the one hand, the argument goes, any "noble thinker" would need an educated wife; on the other hand, one didn't want to end up with a manly woman. The Committee plays it safe: "To all this it may be said that these considerations are too general and remote

The Woman Question

– that woman's most immediate duties relate to maternity, and that her most beautiful mission relates to the dispensing of charities...Suffice it that the system of education proposed cannot make it worse, and may make it better." In other words, it might help and it can't hurt.

Finally, the Committee recommends accepting "the proposal signed by The Honorable Henry W. Sage, of Brooklyn, a member of the Board of Trustees, offering to the Institution the sum of two hundred and fifty thousand dollars, to be paid within three years from the acceptance of the offer, on the condition, to use his exact language, that 'instruction shall be afforded to young women, by the Cornell University, as broad and as thorough as that now afforded to young men.'" The more pressing question for the committee now was how to physically achieve the goal.

To this end, they offered two suggestions for the building. The first plan would consist of buildings adjacent to the campus, including classrooms and houses that would be rented to married professors who would agree to take in female student boarders in a family setting. Vice President Russel strongly opposed the "cottage" plan, fearing a lack of supervision of the young women, saying, "The more I think of the professor-boarding house plan, the less I like it. It sounds well and looks well...but put yourself in the place of the parents of these girls: Is every professor the right sort of man and every professorin the right sort of woman with whom to place young women? As good a person as the Lady Superintendant of Sage would be? Who among them would undertake to prevent the evening appointments and country excursions so demoralizing to both parties?"

The Committee agreed, favoring a plan that would provide maximum supervision of the women, and add a large, beautiful building to central campus. In addition to centrally locating the women, Sage Hall would also provide dining and entertainment space for the single men, students and professors alike, who lived in Morrill Hall, the crowded all-purpose dormitory, library, classroom and laboratory space on the Arts Quad.

A.D. White actually favored the more open system of unsupervised housing for women, but felt that the centralized residence hall would be more acceptable to the conservative Eastern establishment critics. Thus his Committee endorsed the construction of Sage Hall:

> ...a large College Building complete in all respects, with lecture room, special recitation rooms, infirmary, gymnasium, bathing-rooms and study and lodging-rooms for from one hundred and fifty to two hundred lady students – a building which would form a striking architectural feature in its connection with the University.

The advantage of this new plan is that it would admit of

most complete supervision – that it would tend to satisfy the popular mind in this respect and that it would add to the dignity of the College and of the University. The disadvantages are that it would require the furnishings and keeping up of a great establishment. This objection vanishes, however, before the proposed endowment, in addition to the cost of the building...

The modern building would add to the prestige of the campus; and of course, Sage's proposal was explicitly to provide for a women's residence hall.

The report was met, as Russel said, "with an unusual silence" by the press, but once published became the definitive statement regarding the feasibility of coeducation in higher education. Martha Goddard of Hartford, Connecticut, future founder of Goddard College, wrote to A.D. White, "If you were a woman, and had been disgusted, mortified, and exasperated as I have been by the talk of educated men about our capacity, or incapacity, rather, I might make you understand the satisfaction, gratitude, and delight with which I read your Report. As it is you can never know anything about it. Please, may I have another copy?"

Societal change is generational, but men were still arguing against women's education in the 20th century. For example,

The Woman Question

"Applied Eugenics," written in 1918 by Paul Popenoe and Roswell Johnson, blamed coeducation for the white race's peril, opining that "many a college girl of the finest innate qualities, who sincerely desires to enter matrimony, is unable to find a husband of her own class, simply because she has been rendered so cold and unattractive, so overstuffed intellectually and starved emotionally, that a typical man does not desire to spend the rest of his life in her company."

Naturally it has been noted that, without the stipulation that Henry Sage had placed on his gift to Cornell University, it may well have been a long time before women were able to attend the institution. Instead, the trustees moved forward to accept the gift, and planning began for Sage Residential College, a grand state-of-the-art building in its day. The philanthropy that Henry Sage directed toward Sage Hall was required to secure a chance for women to succeed at the university, and like it or not, the Cornell community was enriched by the presence of female students.

Photograph of Sage College
Courtesy of the Division of Rare and Manuscript Collections,
Cornell University Library

Chapter 3: The Experiment of Coeducation

On the sixteenth of May in 1873, Cornell University held a ceremony to commemorate the laying of the cornerstone of Sage Residential College for Women. According to the student newspaper, the *Cornell Era*, the event had not been widely publicized, but had nonetheless drawn educators interested in coeducation. The paper wrote of the attendees who supported the cause, "that this, which may be called formal sanction by the trustees of a most important policy, one that seems hazardous and rash except to the boldest and clearest sighted, deserved, yes, their aid and cheering counsel – their reassurance and blessing." As previously noted, the faculty and male students were largely unconvinced of the wisdom of having women in the classroom.

Local citizens also turned out for the event, and the *Era* records the town's collective luck with the famously unpredictable Ithaca weather: "The fates had never decreed a finer day for any public occasion than this. Not a cloud could be seen, and the sun shone genially, not too warm through an atmosphere so clear that the great range of prospect from the Sage building lay in its greatest possible grandeur and variety before the observer. The ceremony was appointed to take place at 2 o'clock, but long before that time the line of pedestrians and carriages began their ascent of the hill."

The Experiment of Coeducation

Margaret Mooney Milmoe was an Ithaca resident, and when asked to give her favorite remembrances of Sage College, she recalled her illicit presence at the laying of the cornerstone at Sage when she was nine years old. The story illustrates both her pluck and the founders' genuine support of equal education for women. Margaret describes the events of that spring day in her lively memoir:

> I had eagerly watched the unearthing and building of the foundation of Sage, and had looked forward to the day when, as had been announced, there was to be a formal ceremony of laying the cornerstone. My aunt was to attend the exercises in company with a lot of young people and I had expected to go with her. But she persuaded my mother that I was too young to understand it, and would only be in the way. So I was sent to school. Sent to school! On the beautiful day when all the then "fall creekers" dressed in their best were mending their way hill-ward, I could not sit still. I was inattentive, uneasy. I must see the stone laying. I asked to be excused from the room. The school gate was locked, but on one side of the yard a low icehouse which sloped to the ground was close to the fence. I climbed to the top of the fence at this place, scaled the icehouse and slid down the other side. I was free and the way was clear...

The Experiment of Coeducation

I was early, a platform had been laid over the foundation and up upon this I climbed...my hands and face were...streaked with dirt and perspiration but I was supremely happy and sublimely unconscious of everything except that I was there and was going to see the ceremony. The crowd kept gathering and finally a band began to play and a procession came towards me on the platform. I was a bit frightened at first until I saw my friend Mr. Cornell advancing and soon I felt quite at ease...

Just then I caught the eye of my aunt who was horrified...she began gesticulating violently, motioning me to come to her. I decided that she deserved only stony stares from me. When the procession reached me, Mr. Cornell started to lift me down to the ground, but President White with his ever-ready kindness of heart said, "Just let the little girl remain. She is not in the way and it's quite appropriate to have a little girl here." So I felt that I was a part of the show and swelled with pride as I looked at my aunt who I knew was fearfully humiliated...

From what I had been able to understand from the speeches, girls were going to do things that they had never done before and I was one of those girls, and as soon as I was old enough I must go to this college and learn to achieve big things.

The Experiment of Coeducation

Clearly she was the type of female that appealed to the founders. Is it the casual atmosphere of the frontier that this vignette captures, or was the idea of educating women so odd that no one knew quite how to act? In any event, Margaret Mooney did go on to live in Sage Hall, and graduated from Cornell University in 1885. She married Patrick Milmoe in Ithaca in 1891, and the couple raised eight children in Canastota, N.Y., where Margaret stayed active in the Collegiate Alumnae Association of Central New York and the Cornell Alumnae Club.

Andrew Dickson White delivered the opening address, in which he applauded the cause of coeducation and recalled that it had been part of his and Ezra Cornell's original vision for the institution:

> It is now a little more than four years since we met in yonder pleasant village to begin, formally, our work of instruction. At that time ground was taken, both by our honored Founder in his introductory speech, and by the President of the institution in his inaugural address, in favor of the education of young men and young women together in colleges and universities. In Mr. Cornell this idea seemed an instinct. He had enjoyed none of the advantages given in seminaries of advanced instruction; he had been too much immersed in business, to have heard much argument for or against perpetuating in the nineteenth century semi-

The Experiment of Coeducation

monastic arrangements which suited the thirteenth; there was in him, I think, an instinctive love of fair play, an instinctive distrust of new theories to bolster up outworn practices; and these instincts he expressed in that first official utterance, when he declared his hope that women should be educated here as well as young men.

White also remembered Sage's offer on the day of the inauguration ceremonies; he credits the majestic scenery of the region as an inspiration for Sage's philanthropical commitment to the university, saying that, "in his boyhood, he had roamed over these hills and along the shores of yonder lake, and among these gorges and forests about us; all this landscape, which has to you merely a wonderful physical beauty, has to him a consecration."

The President explains the delay in implementing Sage's gift, and also praises Sage's generosity, which in effect must have been difficult to refuse:

> Time passed on. There was a world of hard work to do in that first period of organization; there were heavy loads to carry, struggles to go through, plans to work out with infinite painstaking; and our friend's offer waited. But it was never forgotten, and at last the time arrived, and he came forward to redeem his promise. Time had not weakened his determination, it had but served to ripen it. His gift was

The Experiment of Coeducation

larger than any of us had dreamed of for such a purpose; and today, for this College and yonder Chapel, it stands at three hundred thousand dollars...

White concluded by expressing his admiration for the architecture of the building, comparing it to edifices on other university campuses:

I know of some few more costly, I know of none more beautiful. I trust that the modesty of our architect, Professor Babcock, will not be offended when I say that he has planned for us a building admirably suited to the founder's noble purpose...But comfort and bare utility have not been the only things thought of. As a believer in the possibility of 'sermons in stones,' I rejoice to see that in and about this building there is to be a great deal of crystallized eloquence, very forcible though very quiet, and moreover, perpetual.

Henry Sage spoke next, and voiced his hope that in the future, women's education would enable them to support themselves and their families when necessary, a hope based on his own experience as sole breadwinner for his mother and sisters. Sage noted that "less than thirty years since, in this State, a married woman could not control her own property - not even the wages earned by her own hands." He also stated his belief that women could be educated without radically changing the structure of the patriarchal state, and indeed, that the education of women would serve to fortify that cultural institution:

> It has been wisely said that who educates a woman educates a generation; and the structure which is to be erected over this corner-stone will be especially devoted to the education of women, and will carry with it a pledge of all the power and resources of Cornell University to provide and *forever maintain* facilities for the education of women as broadly as for men.
>
> I am not one of those who believe that the nature and functions of woman, or her most important sphere of duties in this life, are to be essentially changed by education. God established these from the beginning, and his purposes do not change. But I do most earnestly believe that every power he has given her, that every grace and virtue which adorn her nature, that every element of usefulness and helpfulness to herself and others, may be increased without limit by education and culture, and that, in proportion as these are added to her, will our race be elevated and improved…

Sage also voiced his fear that, due to war, emigration and other causes – shipwrecks among them, which had caused his father's death and his family's destitution – there would be not just

The Experiment of Coeducation

impoverished women, but also a population imbalance. He noted that "in Great Britain, the female population exceeds the male by nearly a million and a half!" He suggests that women might rebel, and that education could be the best tool to keep all these women, whose "nature" denied them "legitimate spheres of action," under control:

> Human souls organized and equipped with faculties for every function of life, endowed by our Creator with all the feelings, impulses, and passions of humanity, instinct with vital force, and reaching out for legitimate spheres of action, which, for very important elements of their nature, can never be attained! In such conditions of this vast mass of humanity, what necessity for restraints and limitations; for elevation and purity; for the positive control of moral and intellectual forces over those of the gross animal nature! And how can this result be attained? There is but one answer to the question: By that elevation of character, by that broadening and deepening of the whole nature, which comes from Christian culture and education.

Sage finished by theorizing that, "in thousands of the less masculine pursuits which men now monopolize, women, educated for the work, can succeed as well. And there is manly work in this world for every man in it besides!"

The Experiment of Coeducation

Whatever one's feeling towards manly men and womanly women, it is hard to argue with Henry Sage's aspirations for the future coeds, or with his closing words at the laying of the cornerstone of Sage College:

> When she is completely emancipated from unjust legal shackles, when she is free as man is to seek her own path in life, wherever led by necessity or duty, hope or ambition, when opportunity and aid for culture in any direction are hers, then may we expect to see woman enlarged, ennobled in every attribute, and our whole race, through her, receive impulsion to a higher level in all things great and good!

The corner stone, containing a time capsule, was then laid, as Mrs. Sage read the following sentiments:

> I lay this corner stone, in faith
> That structure fair and good
> Shall from it rise, and thenceforth come
> True Christian womanhood.

Her words would prove somewhat ironic when Ezra Cornell's letter was recovered from the time capsule during the Sage Hall renovation, revealing his true fear for the failure of the institution. Charles Babcock, first architecture professor at Cornell and a founding member of the Architectural Institute of America spoke next, detailing the contents of the box:

The Experiment of Coeducation

1. Parchments bearing the date of the laying of the stone, and the names of the architect and builder.

2. Copies of the *Register.*

3. Laws and documents relating to the University.

4. The *Albany Evening Journal Almanac* of 1873.

5. The *New York Daily Times.*

6. The Ithaca daily papers.

7. *The Era.*

8. A letter addressed by Mr. Cornell "To the Coming Man and Woman."

The founders concluded the program, as A.D. White introduced the ailing Ezra Cornell:

> The corner stone of the Sage College is now duly laid; may God's blessing rest upon the college, upon its benefactors, upon all who throng its walls, upon all who go forth from it! I have now the pleasure of introducing the gentleman who has written the letter, which has been deposited in the stone, to the coming man and the coming woman. I trust it may be a very long time before that letter comes to its address.

Cornell, who would not live to see the building finished, reaffirmed his belief that coeducation was the right thing to do, and reminded the townspeople that it was his intention that the institution be beneficial to his beloved Ithaca community:

> Mr. President, Ladies and Gentlemen:

The Experiment of Coeducation

You will not expect me to undertake to do what I am so little qualified to do – to make a speech; but I rise with pleasure to thank God and our friends, in the name of the Trustees of Cornell University, that this great work goes steadily forward.

Four years ago we met and incorporated the Cornell University. There was a doubt, at least, whether there was not a majority of our Trustees, and a majority of the Faculty that had then been selected for the University, opposed to this work. I cannot say that this was the fact, but it is difficult also for me to say that it was not the fact.

The work is moving forward; and I am now able to assure you that at least a majority, and a very decided majority, of both the Trustees and the Faculty, are in favor of this great experiment, and as for myself, I have the utmost confidence in its success. I regard it as the most important experiment that could be made, not only for the institution, but for our surrounding country. It is important to the citizens of Ithaca, that this experiment should be a successful one…Again thanking our friends for the means that have enabled us to make this rapid progress in this matter of coeducation, and of placing the women of America upon the same footing with the men of America in regard to education, I will close, with the remark that the letter

The Experiment of Coeducation

deposited in the corner stone addressed to the future man and woman, of which I have kept no copy, will relate to future generations the cause of the failure of this experiment, if it ever does fail, as I trust in God it never will.

Was Cornell intentionally vague in his reference to "this experiment"? Despite Cornell's "utmost confidence" in the success of coeducation, historians invariably assumed that the letter specifically addressed the experiment of coeducation.

There wasn't much to Ithaca four years earlier, when the Board of Trustees met in Cornell Library to incorporate Cornell University. The bulk of the population of seven thousand, a village until incorporated as a city in 1888, lived between the inlet to the lake (now a flood-control canal) and downtown, at that time delimited by Green, Aurora and Court (then Mill) Streets. On East Hill, Cascadilla Place was constructed as a water cure sanitarium and school for the education of women doctors and nurses in 1865, on the former site of a cotton mill; Ezra Cornell had contributed to its establishment, but it would soon become home to the early classes of Cornell University students, its faculty and their wives. Down the hill, there were flour and plaster mills powered by the water of Ithaca Falls, and a settlement of mill-workers nearby. In fact, the waterpower of the area, that boasts 150 waterfalls within ten miles of Ithaca, was a vital resource for the early settlers.

The Experiment of Coeducation

At the base of the west side of South Hill, our house was probably built in the 1880's, when our property was still outside of the city limits, and well before electric and gas lines reached our road in the 1930's. Constructed with oak floors and chestnut trim, plaster and lath walls, cedar siding and shake roofing, it's located downhill from a quarry that produced slate for the nascent town's sidewalks. We speculate from the precision of the blasting in the bedrock cellar that it may have belonged to the quarry master, but the house doesn't show up in the Ithaca City Directory until 1890, when a man with a sign painting business in town lived in it.

Up the hill from our house is the old Ithaca and Owego Railroad track, with a culvert over our small creek, and its waterfall and gorge. The rails are gone, and now the rail-bed is used as a hiking and dog-walking trail. The Ithaca and Owego Railroad, opened in 1834, provided a route from Cayuga Lake to the Susquehanna River in Owego and points south. Horses walked in endless circles in powerhouses at the Ithaca terminal, raising and lowering railcars and wagons on two inclined planes between the downtown flats and the tracks on South Hill, and pulled the cars on wooden rails covered with strap iron.

Before the railroads, steamboats were king, and connected Ithaca to the rest of the world via the Cayuga Bridge at the northern end of the lake and the Erie Canal system. By the 1830's, the steamboat *DeWitt Clinton* departed for the Bridge at 6:00 AM

The Experiment of Coeducation

daily, returning home to Ithaca by sunset, and canal boats transported goods up and down the lake; but by the mid-19th century railroads were the chief means of access to and from our "centrally isolated" city. Ezra Cornell used two million of his own dollars to establish two railroads, which eventually provided Ithacans service as far as Geneva, Cortland and Horseheads, with an East Ithaca station near the campus; by 1893 an electric trolley linked the Lehigh Valley station downtown on the west end with the East Hill station.

Visitors to the organizational meeting for Cornell University, on September 5, 1865, would have lacked most of these amenities. The group gathered for the first meeting of the Board of Trustees of Cornell University, and the attendees included the Governor and Lt. Governor of New York, as well as state senators and assemblymen. Their mission was to create an organization to structure the future institution. They would have arrived by train and steamer from points west and north, and perhaps by train from the south; the rail journey from New York City took twelve hours. From the station or landing, they would take a horse-cab downtown, where they had a choice of accommodations in the Ithaca House, the more venerable establishment, no longer standing, or perhaps the newer, now restored Clinton House, a Greek Revival structure with a statewide reputation for its elegant architecture and good service.

The Experiment of Coeducation

The Trustees met in the Cornell Library to elect officers and appoint committees, and most importantly to accept Ezra Cornell's proposal to endow the university by donating funds to buy the state's Morrill Act land scrips, and to present it to the State Comptroller for approval. This controversial proposition allowed Cornell and White to consolidate the state funding with Cornell's endowment, through the profitable sale of timberland that Ezra bought in the Midwest, to create the hybrid university. Part land grant and part privately endowed, the unique institution would become not only an Ivy League liberal arts and sciences college, and one of the first coeducational institutions of higher education in the world, but also the successor to the first agricultural school in the country, the New York State Agricultural College in Ovid, whose trustees were also on Cornell's first Board.

Ezra Cornell purchased his farm on East Hill from Simeon DeWitt in 1857. After Governor Fenton signed the Morrill Act in 1862, Cornell went forward with his plan to donate two hundred acres of his land for the establishment of the university. Cornell's family lived on the farm in a house known as Forest Park, built in 1839 near what is now the intersection of Stewart Avenue and Campus Road. There were no bridges over the gorges; the road to the farmhouse followed the country road to Dryden, then branched off and ended at Forest Park. Ezra's sheep and prize-winning herd of Devon Shorthorn cattle grazed on the hillside. Apart from them

The Experiment of Coeducation

and the spectacular view of the lake, there wouldn't have been much for his visitors to see on their tour of East Hill in 1865.

A few years later, the campus's central quadrangle was already taking shape. A.D. White, a great lover of fine architecture, would eventually amass one of the best collections of architecture books in the country and donate it to Cornell University, along with the other 30,000 books in his library. But White's youthful dreams of a European-style Gothic Revival campus were thwarted by more practical minds, as the original buildings on the Arts Quadrangle were simple but elegant Second Empire structures with Mansard roofs, built from Ithaca bluestone known as Llenroc ("Cornell" spelled backwards) from a nearby quarry. Morrill Hall was built in 1868, White Hall soon after, and McGraw Hall in 1872, and they were known as "Stone Row," facing the western valley and sweeping view of Cayuga Lake.

Once the Board of Trustees had accepted Henry Sage's offer to construct and endow a women's college, the university's first architecture professor, Charles Babcock, was chosen to design Sage Hall, and White's dreams of Victorian Gothic buildings on the campus began to be realized now. White and Sage supervised every aspect of the design, with a dual goal: an architectural masterpiece and a home-like residence for the young women. The building would be the first of several campus structures still gracing the central campus to feature colored brick decoration that emphasized the arches and contours of the buildings, including the nearby Sage Chapel, and the A.D. White House, once home to White and subsequent presidents of the university. White went so far as to import stone carvers from Scotland to embellish the structures with details depicting local flora.

In 1872, Babcock wrote, "I am working all my spare time on the Sage College," and indeed the design process lasted for years. Babcock took inspiration from John Ruskin, whose book *The Stones of Venice* had a great influence on 19th century architecture. In it, Ruskin argued that there was a need for a universal standard of aesthetics to apply to architecture, in order to perfect it. He broke the exercise down into the two "virtues of architecture":

> In the main, we require from buildings, as from men, two kinds of goodness: first, doing their practical duty well; then, that they be graceful and pleasing in doing it; which last is itself another form of duty…

> We have, then, two qualities of buildings for subjects of separate inquiry: their action, and aspect, and the sources of virtue in both; that is to say, Strength and Beauty, both of construction and decoration, in the edifices of men, depends upon our being led by the thing produced or adorned, to

some contemplation of the powers of mind concerned in its creation or adornment.

Ruskin found that the strength of a structure came from the ingenuity of its builder, thus from human creativity. But in decoration, he advocated designs inspired by nature, and thus emanating from the divine:

> So, then, the first thing we have to ask of the decoration is that it should indicate strong liking, and that honestly...But the second requirement in decoration, is that it should show we like the right thing. And the right thing to be liked is God's work, which He made for our delight and contentment in this world. And all noble ornamentation is the expression of man's delight in God's work.

Ruskin's models of decorative brickwork in palatial buildings in Venice were adapted by Babcock for the Sage College design, which has indeed stood the test of time.

Yet Babcock was forced to defend his authority against Ezra Cornell's belief that the architect's role ended with the design, after which the craftsmen took over the project. In a letter to White in February of 1872, Babcock argued for the architectural integrity of the design of the building, saying, "I have the responsibility for producing a building that shall be a credit to the University...I do not wish to be hampered by or compelled to fight with parties who have no knowledge of architecture." Babcock prevailed, and the building was built as he and White envisioned it, although finally smaller than originally planned due to economic constraints.

Anna Botsford Comstock was one of the original inhabitants of Sage Residential College, and wrote about life in Sage in her autobiography, *The Comstocks of Cornell*. Anna Botsford grew up in Cattaraugus County in western New York State, in the hamlet of Otto. She graduated from Chamberlain Institute in nearby Randolph, NY in 1873, and when she expressed an interest in Cornell University, a male colleague told her that the boys at Cornell "'wouldn't pay any attention to the college girls.' I thought about this seriously and finally concluded: 'Cornell must be a good place for a girl to get an education; it has all the advantages of a university and a convent combined.'"

Anna began her studies in 1874, the sixth year of Cornell University's existence. She notes the difficulty of finding lodging in Ithaca, but eventually found a room downtown and a place to board across the street. Like Jennie Spencer before her, she struggled with the uphill walk to campus, writing that "in 1874 there were no sidewalks between my home and the University. I climbed East Hill as best I could, thankful that as a country girl I was accustomed to bad roads."

The Experiment of Coeducation

In the rooming house, Anna's room was "frankly a bedroom," and her housemates were men with rooms off the same hallway. She says, "I was not disturbed by this, for I expected no social relations with gentlemen. Imagine my dismay when, answering a knock at the door, I discovered a tall, dignified man who evidently expected to be invited in. I stood guard firmly..." It simply wasn't done for a young lady to entertain men in her bedroom. Finally the landlady suggested that Anna take another small room as her bedroom and convert the first into a study, where she "might receive callers without embarrassment. When we had made the change it was an attractive room and greatly needed, for there were many callers." Apparently the men at Cornell were interested in the college girls after all.

In the summer of 1875, Anna became engaged to one of the men in her house, but then broke it off, writing that the affair "was too emotional to meet the realities of life." Several Brazilian students also lived in the rooming house, and Anna describes them as "serious, quiet and polite" and sometimes homesick, weeping with her when a letter from her mother made her cry. Despite the warning of Cornell's Vice-President William Channing Russel that the Brazilians had "very different customs," one of them accompanied her to a dance, and Anna recalls that "no Puritan youth could have treated me with more courtesy and respect" than did her Brazilian escort.

The Experiment of Coeducation

Anna Botsford and her family would have received a copy of the pamphlet that the university sent out to prospective Cornell co-eds when Sage College opened its doors, touting the modern amenities of the building, especially its healthful aspects, as well as its opulent features:

> It is a substantial and beautiful structure, having a front of 176 feet, and two wings 162 feet deep, and containing reception rooms, parlors, music rooms, study rooms and bedrooms sufficient for one hundred and twenty ladies. Its position on the University grounds, commanding a view of Cayuga Lake and surrounded by hills and valleys, is one of the most beautiful in the State, and its height, 400 feet above the lake, insures conditions favorable to health. It is heated with steam, lighted with gas, provided with all the modern conveniences, with baths on every floor, with a gymnasium, and a sheltered corridor for walking in bad weather. Adjoining the buildings are ornamental grounds and botanical and other gardens, where lady students can have practical and healthful instruction in the intervals of their studies, under the guidance of the Botanical Professor and his assistants...
>
> The public rooms at the disposal of the students consist of large parlors and reception-rooms, reading and dining-rooms and apartments for literary societies. Private rooms

The Experiment of Coeducation

are arranged in suites, so that every two young ladies have a neat study chamber separated by a permanent screen from their sleeping-room…

The engravings and casts with which the public rooms are decorated have been purchased at Berlin, Paris and London, with the intention of surrounding the students with objects of taste and beauty…

A healthy home and social influence is…exercised upon all the inmates. From time to time, especially in the winter, there are social entertainments and readings of the masterpieces of English authors by various Professors; musical evenings are also given; and every effort is made to diversify the life of study at the College by ennobling entertainments…

Anna's family did not belong to a church; her father had broken with his Methodist past, to his parents' dismay, and her mother was a Quaker. She writes that, "One phase of life in Chamberlain Institute I found unpleasant – the pressure put upon me, mostly by my schoolmates, to "experience religion"; she looked forward to the non-sectarian atmosphere at Cornell. The pamphlet, while confirming that church attendance would be voluntary, also suggests that religious education would be part of the girls' instruction, due to the further munificence of Henry Sage:

The Experiment of Coeducation

Mr. Sage has erected near Sage College, a chapel calculated to accommodate five hundred students. No care has been spared to make it suitable to religious worship. In its whole construction, down to the minutest piece of carved stonework or woodwork, and even to the stained glass in the window, everything has been carefully designed to make the place attractive in all respects...

The University does not compel students to attend these religious services, but every effort is made to attract them, and these sermons have already proved to be powerful means of good. Attendance is entirely voluntary and left to the conscience of each student.

The pamphlet advertised the "Advantages Enjoyed by Lady Students at Cornell University," which seem to be mainly a question of access to the various courses of study and campus facilities. Anna was entitled to the same degree upon completing the same course as "any other student"; and was permitted to use the libraries, whose collections were truly prodigious due in great part to the avid book collecting of A.D. White:

> Now the third in size and probably the second in value among all college and university libraries in the United States, being only surpassed in either of these respects by the libraries of Harvard University and Yale College. There are

The Experiment of Coeducation

at present over 40,000 bound volumes in the Cornell University Library, as shown in the last report of the Librarian...The library has a commodious reading-room in the midst of the books, which is open all day every working day in the year. It is warmed by steam and students studying in it are served with books by the Librarian and his assistants who are glad to give any information required regarding courses of reading, etc.

Women were also allowed to use the laboratories and drafting rooms, to read the periodicals taken by the University, and in short had "the opportunity to profit by instruction, experiments, and demonstrations which each year cost the University the interest on over a million and a half of dollars." Sage College opened for occupancy in September of 1875, although, according to the disapproving Professor Goldwin Smith, "without enough women students to keep ghosts out of dark corners."

Anna Comstock wrote that Sage College was "a fine home for the women students and highly appreciated by those of us who had experienced the difficulties of living in town...My pleasant room was on the north side of the second floor. My roommate was a junior, Minerva Palmer, a beautiful Quakeress, and our companionship proved ideal." The *Cornell Era* described the 14x18 foot student rooms, divided into bedroom and study by a wooden screen: "They are all handsomely fitted with sets of white ash

Drawing Room in Sage College
Courtesy of the Division of Rare and Manuscript Collections,
Cornell University Library

The Experiment of Coeducation

furniture consisting of bed and mattress, wash stand, bureau with mirror, wardrobe, study table, book shelves and chairs. Each study room has a neat and sufficient steam register abundantly equal to the task of warming the study and the annexed bedroom," certainly a welcome amenity in the Ithaca winters. It may be worth reminding oneself that gas lighting, steam heat and indoor plumbing were rare in upstate New York even in the late nineteenth century.

Although the building was located on the central campus, it took some time for the women to be integrated into the student body. Ellen Coit, a Cornellian who wrote about her college days, remembered that the coeds kept a low profile, walking "demurely, as inconspicuous as we could manage, and took seats, always at the very front – probably only three or four of us together to keep each other company." Still, since only thirty women lived in Sage, male students and instructors were encouraged to eat in the College's dining room, with fixed seating arrangements to distribute the men and women.

Cornell student Daniel Sachs, author of a 1955 thesis titled "The Origin and Early Years of Coeducation at Cornell University," notes that, "In these first years of coeducation, there was indeed almost no contact between the sexes. A man incurred the opprobrium of his fellows if he was seen talking to a lady student on campus...they felt constrained to keep up their pose

The Experiment of Coeducation

even in the dining-room: most of the men sat together by themselves, and whenever one of their fellows succumbed to a coed's charm and sat with the girls, a placard was hung on his chair which read, 'One more unfortunate gone to his death. We mourn our loss!'" The professors, however, seem to have enjoyed the arrangement: Sachs tells us that, "after dinner or supper the ladies and gentlemen would go into the gymnasium and dance, or gather around the piano and sing."

The original group of women living at Sage College in 1875, including the freshmen, occupied only the first two floors of the building, and apparently lived a rather unsupervised existence. Anna Comstock recalled an event that illustrates what she called their "college spirit":

> Ruth Putnam came to my room one evening, asserting indignantly that the freshmen were holding a meeting, and she averred something should be done about it. Something was done immediately; water from a pitcher was dashed over the transom, to dampen freshman ardor. But it did not work that way. They made a sortie upon us, and as they outnumbered us, there was a struggle on the stairs and a rumpus in the halls which shocked everybody not in the squabble.

The Experiment of Coeducation

This fracas resulted in the organization of a student government association in Sage College, and a committee was appointed to make rules for our guidance.

Among the rules that the women adopted was to ignore their male acquaintances on campus, since apparently gender relations were such that both men and women preferred to keep the women "invisible":

> These few rules, unanimously adopted, were not unlike the rules of the Cornell Women's Self Government Association of today [1875], except for the restriction that women students should not bow to their men friends on the Campus. We were so few that it was embarrassing to be recognized in the crowds of men while changing classes. As soon as we explained to our friends the reason for ignoring them, they not only accepted the dictum, but confessed relief.

Yet despite the occasional social tensions, it sounds like the early co-eds in general had pleasant and entertaining times in the building; as Anna put it,

> We had a happy social life in Sage that first year. The gymnasium was on the east side and was reached from the front hall by way of a covered porch. We had dances there

every Friday night; sometimes there were girls only, but more often our men friends were invited.

Musicals and readings from Shakespeare and modern American writers by Professor Hiram Corson were part of the social scene at Sage College, and the women also received frequent visits from A.D. White, who gave talks on various subjects, as Anna recalled, "from our proper behavior to the art of the Renaissance." In short, the women's residence became a focal point in the social life of the campus.

Anna Botsford had taken the young instructor John Henry Comstock's entomology course in the fall of 1875, and she admired his teaching, but it was at Sage that her "real acquaintance with Henry Comstock began":

> Men came to Sage for their meals, and we were allowed to invite our friends to sit with us at table. I asked Mr. Comstock and Dan Flannery, class of 1876, one of my preparatory school friends; both were rooming in Morrill Hall. I was told afterwards by the manager of Sage that Mr. Comstock asked if he could sit next to me…We had happy times at meals. We were so gay and laughed so much that we were looked at askance by some representatives of dignity and decorum; but we laughed as we chose.

The Experiment of Coeducation

Anna married Henry in 1878, after he had lost a fiancée – also a Cornell student – to tuberculosis. She dropped out of Cornell after two years, but returned to graduate with a degree in Natural History in 1885. Anna Comstock was the first female professor at Cornell, although the trustees originally removed her title because of her gender. She was reinstated by Liberty Hyde Bailey, but denied full professorship until 1920, two years before she retired.

The "Comstocks of Cornell" were life-long partners in marriage and in exploring the world of entomology, and she pioneered the academic discipline of nature illustration. She wasn't formally trained in art at first, but simply drew the insects she saw under a microscope; after studying wood engraving at Cooper Union, she made over 6,000 plates for Henry's entomology textbooks and reports. Among her other engravings is a view of Sage Hall [*page 128*]. Her classic work, *The Handbook of Nature Study* (1911) is still in print, and credited as an early text encouraging teachers to take their biology students out of the classroom and into the field.

Although Cornell women were originally barred from all extra-curricular activities, this slowly changed, due to their own diplomatic efforts. For example, in January of 1878, a dozen sophomore coeds lobbied to attend their class supper at the Ithaca

The Experiment of Coeducation

Hotel. They felt they were entitled to attend the event, as members of the class who had paid their dues; yet they offered to stay home if "their presence would detract in any way from the enjoyment of the gentlemen of the class." Instead they were unanimously invited to attend, and later the men wrote that "they lent grace to the festal board and a piquant sauce to the bill of fare." The young ladies left before the toasts; still, *The Era*'s account of the dinner created controversy, leading some readers to call it "the last straw," since the class suppers had been a final stronghold of single sex privilege.

Daniel Sachs tells us that "because this action manifested their desire for complete equality with the men...the ladies were warned that, 'If they persist in this apparent desire that they shall be treated as men, they must not be disappointed if they receive the same treatment as men; in short, they must stand in crowded classrooms, content themselves as best they can with poor seats, must drill or present a substitute, must expect no favoritism from the professors, and must not exclaim when things are said or done in their presence which might be expected to shock more sensitive beings.'"

The Era complained in 1879 that, "the ladies are now in all literary societies...they belong to all the technical clubs, and in a few years, no doubt, will hold this pen which now attacks them. Is

The Experiment of Coeducation

not this going too far? Are not the peculiar advantages of association of men with men weighty enough to cause a need here of some organizations not wholly coeducational in character?" To this day, of course, there are single sex student organizations on the Cornell campus; still, times were slowly beginning to change.

Sachs notes that, as the coed population changed from the original women, who were somewhat older than their male counterparts, to freshman girls who "were interested in a life at Cornell outside the classroom," the younger men were correspondingly more open to friendly relationships with the female students. A letter to *The Era* in 1879 recorded the changing climate on campus, saying that "Now it is quite the fashion to walk from building to building in company with a young lady; to pour forth the usual bosh-bosh for her entertainment; and to solace oneself during the hour by sending her an occasional note."

Free to choose their lodgings, most women lived downtown, in rooming houses or with relatives, and even those who lived in Sage College were minimally supervised. Moreover, they resented the idea of enforced supervision; as Florence Kelley, one of those early coeds put it, "We were a serious, self-conscious body of pioneers, in no need of student government or any other." But in April of 1879, A.D. White told the women that the Board of Trustees was considering more stringent rules of management for the building, including hiring a woman as "Warden" to supervise

The Experiment of Coeducation

the women. More importantly, the Board proposed to require all the women students to live in Sage College. Even *The Era* protested the action, commenting that, "The young ladies for whom the Sage endowment was given have too much purpose in being here, and are too womanly, to need the iron boarding-house rules in regard to social intercourse with their gentlemen friends." Nevertheless, the Board went forward with the changes.

The women held a mass meeting in Sage Hall to consider a protest, and formed the "Sage College Association," an attempt at substituting self-governance, like Anna Comstock's class had done, for the imposition of a matron. Daniel Sachs tells us that the coeds "promulgated a set of regulations which they hoped would be considered 'sufficient provision against any future possible trouble'…The rules…provided for a 10:00 PM curfew, enjoined the ladies from walking, lounging, or sitting about on the grounds after dark, and set up machinery for the investigation and penalization of infractions."

Not all the women agreed to the self-imposed curfew. In his autobiography, A.D. White recalled being faced with a delegation of coeds who argued that they should be as free as the men to come and go from their dormitory. He told them that "it was like their right to walk from the campus to a beautiful point opposite us on the lake. The right they undoubtedly had, but insurmountable obstacles were in the way; and I showed them that public opinion

The Experiment of Coeducation

was an insurmountable barrier to the liberties they claimed." Was he giving in to pressure from Henry Sage or others on the Board, or outside the university? In any event, as more women entered Cornell University, and fewer of them chose to live at Sage College, the Board of Trustees took action in 1884 to make residency compulsory for all female students who did not have relatives in town.

Sachs writes, "It pained Mr. Sage and the other trustees to see only twenty-five girls in a building designed for one hundred and twenty. Unless Sage College was filled to capacity, it would have to be put to some other use, because such an expensive building could not stand idle. Since it was thought that the public was suspicious of the moral standards prevailing at Sage College, the Trustees, at the behest of Mr. Sage, hired Mrs. Agnes Derckheim as Lady Directress of Sage College, to give tone and character to the place in the eyes of the public." The next half-century did little to dispel the notion that the university should function *in loco parentis* – at least for women.

As Sachs understood in 1955, this was a turning point for coeducation at Cornell: "The new plan, which was to characterize the life of the Cornell coed from that day to this [*and in fact until 1969*] was entered into lightly by President White. He had been considering this move for two or three years, but had held back from putting it in force until all other methods could be tried…Although he was not enthusiastic over this measure, he thought little harm could be done by giving the plan a fair trial…he thought of the new rule not as an indictment of the women's previous conduct, but simply as a practical way of meeting a serious administrative difficulty." So – it might help and it couldn't hurt, just like White's final argument to the Board for coeducation in the first place. But in this case it did hurt, because the women were being forced to pay for luxuries that many couldn't afford, in order to maintain Henry Sage's dream of their perfectly confined space, their gilded cage.

The text of the protest that the women wrote is a model of diplomacy, but their resentment of the proposal comes through in the italics (theirs):

> We, the undersigned, women of the Alumni body of Cornell University, believing *compulsion in regard to boarding-places* and *the making of any arbitrary distinction between two classes of students* to be unnecessary, unwise, unjust, do hereby respectfully protest against the law enacted by the Executive Committee of the Board of Trustees, July 3rd, 1884, by which residence at Sage College was made compulsory upon women students; and we beg leave to lay before you the reasons for our belief and consequent protest.

The Experiment of Coeducation

They set forth at length their philosophical positions, and also refute the arguments of the Board point by point: First, the women argue that the law is unnecessary, since neither of two necessary conditions existed: that women were unfit to choose homes for themselves, or that the University was in such a financial position that "rendered imperative the maintenance of a building according to its original purpose rather than the personal freedom of all its students." The women point to the complete lack of a history of discipline imposed on them in the past as a vindication of their fitness to control themselves, whether living in or out of Sage College. As to the second condition, that the institution was financially constrained to keep Sage College a residence hall for women, they note the general university policy of adapting other campus buildings to different purposes as the need arose – Sage College being the sole exception.

Second, the women assert that the law is unwise, and that the dormitory system, "whose fitness for the natures and needs of young persons is held in grave doubt by many of the most advanced educators of our country...[be] *forced* upon one class of students." They quote the "Report of the Committee on Organization" presented to the Cornell University Trustees in 1866, which compared a dormitory system, under which the student is "kept, or rather supposed to be kept, under surveillance of the University authorities," to a system that considered a

The Experiment of Coeducation

student's housing outside the "proper function of a university." The report found that a student would be "best left to make arrangement for his lodging as any other person coming for a time into the town would do, subject to certain general regulations by the University...the Committee believe the latter system the more sound in theory and the more satisfactory in practice." Thus the officially adopted university policy regarding housing was breached with the new requirement for women to live in Sage College.

The women go on to quote a report from a committee on co-education at Harvard that claimed that: "The seclusion of the college dormitory is the only reminiscence, among ourselves, of the old cloister." They also quote the president of the University of Michigan: "In general we have disapproved of dormitories, when they are not absolutely necessary. We count it a great good fortune that we have not been obliged to have them. The problems of discipline are vastly simplified by the abolition of them"; and the president of the University of Wisconsin who noted ironically that: "Colleges without dormitories are more easily governed than those with them...The feelings of parents, however, are met by our Ladies' Hall. With no very good reason, they feel safer about their daughters when they are in the Hall." Other presidents of coeducational institutions agreed that a combination of the two options offered the best solution for the students and the institutions.

The Experiment of Coeducation

In addition, the protest includes individual testimonials, for example one from a woman who had lived in Sage College until "sufficient accommodations in private families were available" and found the latter "infinitely the most desirable method of living." Another coed, who lived her entire undergraduate career at Sage, wrote, "I have taught in a Young Ladies' College, and I know just the influence that restrictions and espionage have upon girls...with the partial removal of responsibility for acts comes a lack of self-control...Independence in thought and reasoning seldom exist without independence of action. I would never send a girl to Sage under the new regime." Another female graduate wrote that the "privileges of Cornell, with the old liberty as to mode of life, have attracted a class of women to whom dictation in matters which beyond a question they were best fitted to arrange for themselves, is irksome in the extreme."

Third, the report argues that the law is unjust in that it raises an artificial barrier to women directly in opposition to Ezra Cornell's intent for all to benefit from his university equally; that it "deprives one class of student – a class which has not merited the deprivation – of personal liberty in the matter of residence"; and that while "by declaration 'women are admitted to the university on the same terms as men,'...by this law a distinction *is* made between the terms on which they are admitted and those on which all other students are admitted; and this distinction is one which during their whole University course subjects them to restrictions to which no other class of students is subject." Indeed, Cornell's well-known slogan, "Freedom with Responsibility" ceased to apply to its female students in 1884, and the situation remained the same until 1969, when a new generation of activists procured the end of the curfew in the women's dorms.

In its final pages, the women's report documents the growth in housing near the university, and the establishment of a trolley system, which had made it entirely possible for women to find lodging within a reasonable commute to campus. They dispute the Trustees' claim that they were being offered a good deal at Sage Hall by paying only what it cost the University, with the twofold argument that, "the furnishing of accommodations at cost does not make it easier for one to use them, if the scale of cost is beyond one's means. It would even appear that the fact of the inmates' paying only for what they use should be a reason for not compelling students to board at Sage College, since they do not thereby make it more successful financially." While the university offered special consideration for women of "actual and special hardship," the protest argues that "many women, who if permitted to live in a modest though entirely comfortable way, could meet the expense of a partial or entire University course, would find it practically impossible to incur the expenses entailed by luxurious surroundings." In addition, they assert, these women would either

The Experiment of Coeducation

be forced to accept a gift to be applied to luxuries, which would be morally unacceptable to them, or to receive loans, placing "an unwarrantable burden on future years."

The protest also speaks to the question of the health of women residing in Sage College and elsewhere. Out of forty-two responses, only one notes an ill effect on her health as a result of her residential situation, and this was "the case of [a woman] who resided at Sage College four years, and, occupying a room on the third floor to lessen expenses, incurred permanent injury to her health by reason of the many flights of stairs." Other women cite the stressful nature of life in a dormitory as an adverse health effect of living in Sage Hall, and reject the Trustee's assertion that unless they lived in Sage Hall they would end up paying higher rents in private homes, pointing out that this was not the case in other coeducational university communities.

Finally, the protesters address the last argument of the Trustees, who wrote that, "If it be said that young women equally with young men, while students in the University, should be free to choose whether they will live in a University building or not, it may be answered simply, that no such provision has ever been made for young men. If it were, the Trustees would doubtless require such privileges to be used here, as sundry other universities in the old world and the new have required such privileges to be used." The women remind the Trustees that, "In the early days of

The Experiment of Coeducation

its existence the University, yielding to the necessity of circumstances, did make provision for the lodging of young men. Cascadilla was fitted up as a dormitory and was stated by the authorities to afford as good accommodations as were afforded by any college within the United States. Residency in this dormitory was not compulsory. It was expressly stated that the system employed by 'sundry other universities in the old world and the new' was not considered wise or desirable, and hence that their example would not be followed, except in so far and so long as the convenience of the students made it necessary." The protest adds that Cascadilla Hall was subsequently given up as a dormitory and adapted for other purposes.

In sum, the women, while recognizing "that Sage College is a beautiful building, and that no such munificent provision has ever been made for lady students in any university," claim that "a gift is by its nature for the advantage of those to whom it is given, and that to adapt the recipients of a gift to the gift, instead of adapting the gift to its recipients, is a contraversion of common usage." While they wanted to keep Sage College as a residential option for the roughly half of the women students who preferred it, they strongly rejected the proposal to make residence in Sage compulsory.

The Board of Trustees passed their proposal over the objections of the women, since the real problem for the University

The Experiment of Coeducation

was financial, not the prospect of "future possible trouble." The policy they adopted created a campus whose student body and social character were shaped by the living restrictions placed on its female undergraduates, as well as by the ratio of three males for every female undergraduate on campus, due to lack of "beds for women" until 1969.

Yet the women of Cornell were grateful for their chance to study at the University. *A Tribute to Henry W. Sage* was published in 1894 to express their admiration for the man who built and endowed Sage Hall, and to review the accomplishments of the early female graduates of the university. The survey is interesting, demonstrating a pragmatic approach to women's progress that contrasts with the lofty ambitions of the early feminists:

> In following the career of the women graduates of the University as is done in brief outline in the following list, three facts at once stand out clearly; the majority teach for a longer or shorter period; a large number marry and generally the record ceases with marriage; comparatively few have no record and those in some cases were married immediately after graduation or could not be reached to gain information concerning them. Not less plain are the inferences to be drawn.
>
> Of those who have yielded the best fifteen or twenty years of

their life to rearing children we may not expect great achievement in other directions, and but few of the women graduates who have thus devoted their lives have passed the period when this is their chief duty. In later life they may pick up the broken threads and carry on activities of other kinds. Some of the women who have not had children have thrown the force of their character into work which is recorded and which if carried to completion will be of great value. A few women who have children but are in their environment and in the sympathetic cooperation of the husband exceptionally placed, are able to carry on a professional or a student's life.

When we look at the record and think of those women who are thrown upon their own resources, who must be both supporter of the family and mother of the children, then we know what the training of a university must mean to them...

Anna Comstock was one of the female Cornell graduates who went on to do academic work, but juggled her home-life and professional career. While women now excel in many academic fields, as well as in industry and business, the choices they face still challenge women who work outside the home. At the same time, slowly but surely, women's choices have expanded. Even the relative lack of enthusiasm for feminism among young women

The Experiment of Coeducation

today may reflect their perception of gender equality in their modern world, though the statistics don't bear that out.

Ironically, Henry Sage, the person who was arguably most responsible for coeducation at Cornell, also helped to impose a system of guardianship on the young women that became increasingly restrictive. It stayed that way until the revival of feminism in the 1960's. Marcia Feingold, a sophomore at Cornell in 1950, recalls circulating a petition among first and second year women to have the curfew raised from 10:30 to 11:00 on weekdays. In a letter to the *New York Times* of June 18, 2010 (in response to an article about Saudi women fighting for limiting their rights), she notes that, "Sadly, there were many women (we called them 'girls' back then) who objected. Too much freedom, they said! They feared that they'd feel social pressure to stay out later than they wanted...and because of this they asked the university to restrict them – and all women along with them. How much longer until women (and men) can take full responsibility for their own lives?" Sage's legacy extended to my freshman year in 1968, when residents of the all-female dormitories on North Campus lived under the 10:30 PM curfew on weeknights, after which the entrances to the halls were locked whether everyone was inside or not. In the spring of '69, the curfew was abolished, due to the successful efforts of senior class women.

The novelist Thomas Pynchon, a Cornell alumnus, wrote an

The Experiment of Coeducation

introduction to Richard Fariña's *Been Down So Long It Looks Like Up to Me*, based loosely on the author's undergraduate years at Cornell. Writing in 1983, Pynchon reminds us that, "1958, to be sure, was another planet. You have to appreciate the extent of sexual repression on that campus at the time." In addition to the curfews for women, landlords were encouraged to report the presence of female students in Collegetown apartments. Pynchon tells us that "This extraordinary meddling was not seriously protested until the spring of 1958, when, like a preview of the '60's, students got together on the issue, wrote letters, rallied, demonstrated, and finally, a couple of thousand strong, by torchlight in the curfew hours between May 23 and 24, marched to and stormed the home of the University president," resulting in Fariña's and three other upperclassmen's suspension, and then reinstatement – the cultural background for his iconic novel, published in 1966.

In the end, Sage Hall holds a mixed legacy for women at Cornell: it gave them access to a world-class university, while making every effort to keep them in their "women's place" on campus. Sage also provides the backdrop for a more disturbing story, one that indicates the difficulty of adhering to the founders' vision after their passing, with Ezra dead and A.D. White physically absent. As Carol Kammen notes in *Part and Apart: the Black Experience at Cornell, 1865-1945*, "The earliest black women at

The Experiment of Coeducation

Cornell lived in Sage College, but in 1907 questions arose about their presence there and, later, in Sage Annex. The issue came up again in 1911 and was resolved by invoking the university's charter: all facilities at the university were open to all students. Later, however, the university's official response changed. A determined dean of women succeeded in keeping black women out of university housing for at least a decade. In those years, even when their parents and others complained, the university's response is disappointing: exclusion from the dormitories, the president and dean asserted, was to protect black women from an uncomfortable situation." This restriction on black women mirrors the imposition of mandatory campus housing for the white women; it was clearly not for the women's comfort, but rather for the appearance of conventional propriety at the university. Like many of the social reforms of the 19th century, progress in coeducation stagnated in the early 20th, as the world suffered from devastating warfare.

Still, the educational experiment opened unknown opportunities for the early coeds. Emma Sheffield was Cornell's first woman graduate in 1873, and Jane Datcher the first African American woman to graduate from Cornell, in 1890; women now number close to half of the university's undergraduate students, and a quarter of the undergrads are minority students. Much more racially diverse and freer in many ways, today's campus reflects the

The Experiment of Coeducation

social changes of American culture in the last century and a half. Housing for Cornell freshmen is still structured; a few years ago controversy surrounded the administration's decision to require all frshmen to live in the same housing area, barring them (but only for that first year) from the various ethnic houses for minorities that have grown on campus in the post-60's decades.

Now all university housing is coeducational, and all students are free to exercise their "freedom with responsibility," in accordance with Cornell University's motto. The wardens of Sage Hall are long gone, but the beautiful structure Henry Sage provided for the coeds' physical comfort still affords an expansive view of the campus and lake from its vantage point high on the hill, in its new incarnation as the Johnson Graduate School of Management – and a woman was president of the first graduating class of MBA's to use the building in 1998!

Engraving of Sage College by Anna Comstock

Courtesy of the Division of Rare and Manuscript Collections,

Cornell University Library

Chapter 4: The Preservation Question

I returned to Ithaca in 1990 as a doctoral candidate in Romance Studies, the charmingly named department that includes my major, French Literature. At the time, Cornell's Graduate School offices were situated in Sage Hall. Along with those offices, the shabby first floor housed "The Henry," a large room used for registration and other events for grads, and a laundromat and vending machines for the visiting scholars who inhabited rooms on the upper floors. The building showed many signs of wear from its 120 years of use, and no one had any idea that it would soon undergo a miraculous transformation to emerge as the new home of the Johnson Graduate School of Management, one of the top business schools in the country. The renovated building is as much a state-of-the-art facility as the Sage Residential College had been in its day.

Bob Stundtner arrived in Ithaca a decade earlier. He returned to Corning, NY in 1972, after his discharge from the Navy, having served in the Philippines during the Vietnam War, to find himself homeless from the devastation caused by Hurricane Agnes. But there was rebuilding to be done, and Bob helped his father Harold start up an electrical contracting business. He subsequently attended SUNY Oswego, graduating *Magna Cum Laude* with a psychology degree in 1976. In 1977, Harold ran as

The Preservation Question

the Democratic candidate for mayor of Corning, and narrowly lost. He asked Bob to move back to Corning to help with the business, so that he could focus more energy on another election bid. After the sitting mayor slashed property taxes to improve his election chances, Harold lost the 1979 election in a landslide, freeing Bob to look for job opportunities elsewhere.

In early 1980, Bob took a position in Cornell's Facilities Services Department and bought our house on the South Side of Ithaca. His memories of those early years on campus include his interactions with countless campus characters, and hundreds of maintenance projects large and small, even the heroic removal of 40 cubic yards of pigeon guano from the tower of McGraw Hall. Rewarded for his work ethic and "people skills," Bob moved up the ladder to become a maintenance analyst, and then a project manager in the Facilities Department. As of this writing, Bob is Director of Capital Project Management and has devoted over 30 years of his life to Cornell University.

From 1990 until its completion in 1996, Bob managed a major asbestos removal and infrastructure project in the Chemistry Department's Baker and S.T. Olin Laboratories. Baker Lab opened in 1923, and S.T. Olin was added on to it in 1967. Olin's tall profile had created a ventilation problem for Baker, which was recirculating a portion of its own exhaust. The $27 million renovation addressed that problem, upgrading the electrical and fire protection systems and improving the energy efficiency of the old air handling and electrical systems by 30%.

Bob and his project coordinator Sharon Wargo, one of many female colleagues Bob has mentored in his career, had offices in the department while the work was being done. Floor by floor, the contractors relocated the professors and their research groups in order to remove the asbestos, and then to gut and replace the mechanical and electrical systems. It took two weeks to move two professors and their groups out of a given floor and into a temporary space, and two and a half months more until they could move back into their original territory, enabling them to continue their work during the course of the renovation. Bob's project team hit every deadline without disrupting the occupants on the other floors of the building, a feat not unnoticed by his supervisors.

In February of 1996, while still completing the Baker/Olin renovation, Bob was chosen by Eric Dicke, then Director of Facilities Planning, and Steve Wright, Director of Planning, Design and Construction, to lead Cornell's project team for the transformation of Sage Hall. Samuel C. Johnson was the fourth generation to lead S.C. Johnson and Son, Inc., a self-described "family company since 1886" based in Racine, Wisconsin. Sam Johnson was also a Trustee Emeritus at Cornell University, his alma mater. In 1984, Johnson and his wife Imogene (whom he met at Cornell) made a $20 million endowment gift to the S.C. Johnson

The Preservation Question

Graduate School of Management, named after Johnson's great-grandfather; their later gifts to the university established the Center for Sustainable Global Enterprise and created a beautiful new facility for the Cornell Laboratory of Ornithology. The Johnsons were forward-thinking people and good friends to Cornell.

The university had decided to use Johnson's gift to move JGSM from its cramped, outdated home in Malott Hall into a new facility constructed inside the historic façade of Sage Hall. The project manager originally assigned to Sage had declined to take on the daunting job, which was scheduled to begin in April. The Baker-Olin project would be finished by the end of December. Bob wasted no time in team building, sending an e-mail to Alan Merton, Dean of the Johnson School, in February:

Dean Merton:

I was hoping to introduce myself to you last Thursday at the Chemistry luncheon, but on my way over to do so, I was intercepted by the Chair of the Department's Building Committee. I'm managing the mechanical and safety renovations to Baker and S.T. Olin, and he was experiencing a problem that required my immediate attention.

You are probably aware that I have been proposed to join your team for Sage as project manager for the construction phase. Earl Peters invited me to the luncheon so that I could meet you and we also thought you might like to tour our project. I'm sorry that time and circumstances didn't permit that, but if you, John McKeown, and/or

The Preservation Question

Prof. Libby [*Robert Libby was Chair of the Johnson School's Building Committee*] are interested, I would be glad to give you a tour.

I found your talk very interesting and was intrigued with your efforts to improve the MBA program by drawing upon resources outside your own faculty. I have been toying with an idea for a graduate seminar in research facility design using the Baker/Olin project as an example of the issues and process. While listening to your description of the twelve-month program for people with advanced degrees in science and engineering, I was thinking that many of those students might be interested in such a seminar.

If, as you stated, many of them are pursuing a Masters of Business Administration because they want to become managers, one of the more challenging issues they will encounter is facilities management. That premise must have some resonance with you as you take the Sage project forward.

As you know, we have some outstanding facilities planning, design, and management resources on campus and access to more specialized resources through our consultants and professional affiliations. I believe those resources could be of value to your MBA programs. If you think there might be some opportunities to collaborate, please let me know and I'll propose a meeting with my colleagues for exploratory discussions.

In any event, I look forward to meeting you and working with you, the faculty, and the staff of the Johnson School in bringing the Sage project to fruition.

Regards,

Bob

The Preservation Question

More than one architectural firm had competed to design a new home for the Johnson School, but Dean Merton wasn't satisfied with any of the early proposals. He hired César Pelli, from New Haven, to evaluate the sites that Cornell was considering for the new facility, none on the central campus. Eric Dicke determined from this study that there was insufficient space at those locations. Finally, the university decided to offer Sage Hall to the Johnson School, and that triggered another round of interviews with architects. Dean Merton's charge to the competing firms was simple: "Dazzle me." Eventually the Hillier Group of Princeton was successful in winning the commission, with Alan Chimacoff as design principal.

An alumnus of Cornell's Architecture Department, Chimacoff knew the history of the building, designed by Charles Babcock, Cornell's first architecture professor, and researched the inspirations for the original design. In his September 1998 presentation at the dedication of the renovated Sage Hall, he noted that "the school's quest for a new facility merged with the university's simultaneous desire to revitalize the dying, dismal Gothic hall – to reassert its prominence in the campus and honor its historic significance to the university as the first building to house women and educate them on an equal footing with men."

Chimacoff's presentation noted the dilapidated condition of the building. Ongoing changes to the structure had compromised its integrity, and the passing of time had dimmed its former glory. The Hillier Group was constrained by the Ithaca Landmark Preservation Commission, which would approve their design, to adhere to the national guidelines set by the U.S. Secretary of the Interior for additions to historic buildings. Those guidelines mandate that the addition must be:

> Compatible but identifiably different from the original to preserve the "story of the building," and be accurate to the timeline of history. Above all, do not replicate historic detail, nor try to obscure the sequence of events.

Chimacoff explained that the new exterior architecture is:

> Based on a thematic analysis of the motifs of the original building, with an appropriate 'interpretive' compatibility of old to new – without replication of historic detail...Seeking additional thematic guidance, where necessary, the architects referred to the original building's inspiration in the University Museum at Oxford.

Chimacoff's team studied the Oxford Museum, with its Victorian Gothic towers, that had influenced Prof. Babcock's design for Sage Hall. In particular, the open court and glass-roofed atrium of the new design echo the "diamond patterned lamella roof structure" of the Dinosaur Hall of the Museum. The Hillier

The Preservation Question

architects found their own inspiration for what the building would become, as recalled in Chimacoff's presentation:

> The most startling architectural feature of the Oxford Museum is the Dinosaur Hall. Elaborately Gothic "to the nines," the room soars to its filigree-textured glass roof where overlapping patterns of rectangular and diamond grids at a very fine scale enclose the hall to the sky with an amazing delicacy. The hall is an enclosed court surrounded by a relatively narrow band of rooms, some classrooms, some offices. The similarity to the arrangement of the original Sage Hall is noteworthy…In considering the scheme for the reconstruction of Sage, clearly the enclosed court was conceived under the influence of Oxford.
>
> The design of the structure and enclosure of the Sage Hall atrium roof is a reinterpretation in strictly modern terms of the geometric characteristics of the lacy detail of the Oxford roof. Our objective was to create similar filigree, compatible with the Gothic world of Sage without either using or copying the Gothic details. The structure had to be light and the ensemble of structure and skylight framing delicately textured. To achieve this there are two separate but visually integrated systems. The diamond patterned roof structure is a "lamella" of structural steel members acting as sloped trusses – "slenderized" by a secondary system of

steel tension cables. Placed above the structural layer is a conventional skylight system set in a rectilinear pattern coordinated visually to overlap the diamond pattern of the steel structure at the crossing points. The visual effect of the two systems in concert is a large-scaled version of the Oxford filigree.

The Johnson School had determined that it needed to increase the building's area from 80,000 to 145,000 gross square feet, and Hillier's plan was to excavate a new basement and expand the building eastward, while creating a new front entrance onto East Avenue, the busiest road on campus. The east addition would house the library, on the site of and designed to evoke the conservatory where the early coeds had studied botany, while lecture halls were located in the basement. A real-time trading and research center and an executive education center were highlights of the new facility, and the centerpiece was the three-story atrium.

Alan Chimacoff invoked the 14th century English mathematician William of Occam's "Principle of Parsimony," known as Occam's Razor, as the guiding principle of the design, and described the design process as "putting my bone structure and cardiovascular system in the body of my 12 year old daughter":

From the simple decision to relocate the Johnson Graduate School of Management to Sage Hall flowed a torrent of

The Preservation Question

complexities. That simple decision necessitated reconstructing an entire new building within the 19th century walls of the original, expanding it with new construction to the east and excavating an entire new basement level...a temporary "exoskeleton," an exterior perimeter structure surrounding and supporting the exterior walls and mansard roofs to be preserved, had to be constructed to enable building a new building within the shell...Occam's Razor (perhaps more appropriately in today's terms, Occam's Laser) says that *one should not increase, beyond what is necessary, the number of entities required to explain anything.*" Complementary to this is the (Sherlock) Holmesian explanation of his method of solving a crime, to wit: Eliminate the impossible; whatever remains, however improbable, is the solution.

Applied to Sage Hall and its complexity, one might say that both Occam's Razor and the method of Sherlock Holmes have been in effect. The solution, not to a crime, but to an architectural problem of enormous puzzlements and obscurities, in effect eliminated the impossible by establishing a few strong thematic principles and as a consequence was guided, almost inevitably, through the morass of conundrums and unimaginable complexities to a correct solution. The simplest explanation of the cause of

The Preservation Question

such complexity remains the decision to locate the Johnson School in Sage Hall.

Chimacoff defended the placement of the business school in the historic building in two ways: first, its central campus location humanizes business and management by its association with the core of the university; and second, it reminds the "ivory tower" that the citizens it educates will largely be engaged in commerce when they join the larger society after their matriculation. He summed up the technical difficulties of the project in a few lines, but these represented serious engineering problems: the support of the exoskeleton during the gutting of the building; underpinning the original, preserved west end of the building; adjusting the original 14 floor elevations within a 2-4 floor building for nearly complete accessibility; and fitting new HVAC systems into the old building dimensions.

Chimacoff also defended the renovation's fidelity to the original building, as it incorporates historical references into the new design to tell the story of how the original building came to be. There was a reason for his defensive stance, since there had been some challenges from local preservationists to the radical renovation of the building.

Ithaca is a special community, whose bumper stickers proclaim it to be "10 square miles surrounded by reality." In 1995

The Preservation Question

the city's Democratic Socialist mayor was a former professor of Electrical Engineering at Cornell, Ben Nichols. He feuded with the university over its voluntary donations to the city, arguing that the tax-exempt institution should do more for the city in exchange for services that the city provided free of charge, like firefighting. Cornell was giving $140,000 a year to the city, and Nichols felt that amount was low, considering that other Ivy League schools generally give more to their respective communities.

The city began attempting to leverage more money from the university by withholding building permits for construction projects, on the grounds that the university was not in compliance with the city's zoning requirements for parking. According to the *Cornell Chronicle* of 1/19/95, Hank Dullea, Cornell's Vice President for University Relations, told the Ithaca Rotary Club on January 11 that, "City of Ithaca officials are 'holding the university hostage to the building permit process' by denying a permit for necessary renovations to Upson Hall and to future building projects unless Cornell contributes as much as an additional $2.56 million to city coffers." Subsequently, Bob found himself in the middle of the controversy when the city denied the building permit for the final phase of the Baker Lab renovation on February 1. As he told the *Daily Sun* on March 2, "We've been working with the city building department and the fire chief for a few years on these upgrades to meet current environmental regulations. The Baker project meets

The Preservation Question

code requirements and does not change use or increase the number of people in the building. All the work is related to repairing and upgrading old equipment, thus parking should not have been an issue." The delay meant that the window of opportunity closed for completing major work in Baker during the summer, when the building was least occupied.

The city's tactics of putting a freeze on building permits hurt Cornell, but they hurt the community as well, as reported in the *New York Times* on May 2, the day after 300 local construction workers marched on Ithaca City Hall to protest the mayor's and City Council's actions. One of the marchers was quoted as saying, "This is extortion, and I'm surprised it's legal." Local union leaders said that, "at least 70% of their workers are out of work because of the delay in major Cornell projects." Local reaction was mixed, but most people in Ithaca appreciate what the presence of Cornell and Ithaca College means to our "centrally isolated" town, the difference between our vibrant multicultural community and a typically sleepy upstate small town.

In what the *Ithaca Journal* called "an unexpected turnaround" on June 1, Ben Nichols announced that he would issue building permits for three large projects, including Baker/Olin, giving little reason for his decision. Behind the scenes negotiations ensued, and eventually, under a new President,

The Preservation Question

Cornell did raise the level of its voluntary contributions to the City of Ithaca.

Different town-gown tensions were revealed in the permit process for the Sage Hall project. Cornell University had gone to the city early in the design process for the Sage renovation, and the Ithaca historic building preservation community was consulted in the process of granting permission to radically alter one of the oldest and most iconic buildings on the Cornell campus, a designated local landmark since 1990. When the university applied for a building permit for the project, it triggered a State Environmental Quality Review to assess the impact of the renovation on the historic structure, and on the Ithaca and Cornell communities.

The city's Planning and Development Board designated itself the lead agency to perform the City Environmental Quality Review, and met with the Ithaca Landmark Preservation Commission (ILPC) to discuss the plan for Sage Hall. To meet national guidelines, the design had to make the new parts of the building facing East Avenue easily distinguishable from the historic structure. Ed Franquemont, then President of Historic Ithaca, a non-profit preservation group, was an influential supporter of the project, which was approved by the ILPC and the city's Planning and Development Board.

The Preservation Question

A permit was issued on May 31, and work began on Sage Hall. But there were principled people opposed to the design, concerned that the building would lose its "her-story," including K.C. Parsons, author of the definitive history of the Cornell campus, and Michael Tomlan, Historic Preservation Planning Program Director in Cornell's Planning Department, and his wife Mary, Chair of the ILPC. Barbara Ebert, a lecturer in Cornell's City and Regional Planning Department, led the charge against the project. She enlisted the help of the Heritage Coalition, a Syracuse-based non-profit organization of which she was a member, to sue the city for granting the building permit for the project on the grounds that the project was not properly reviewed. They succeeded in getting an injunction to temporarily prohibit any work on the exterior of the building.

Alan Chimacoff described the ordeal, and countered the opposition's arguments, at the dedication of the building:

> The reconstruction of Sage Hall for the Johnson Graduate School of Management was accomplished amid controversy over historic preservation. The focus of argument and acrimony was whether the heart, soul and integrity of the building was being destroyed by the extent of removal of original historic fabric necessitated by the reconstruction.

The Preservation Question

Our process began by seeking the participation and guidance of those in Ithaca most knowledgeable and passionate about questions of historic preservation. At our earliest project organization and design meetings a number of folks listened and participated as we discussed the university's program necessities and architectural preferences, the requirements of the building and life-safety codes, the view and position of the Ithaca Building Inspector.

During the course of the project two groups of preservation architects contributed significantly their research, professional guidance, and profound analytical and technical expertise. Our structural engineer, Robert Silman [*also a Cornellian*], in many ways the sage (no pun intended) of historic structures, led us into realms of discussion over the Guidelines of the Secretary of the Interior as they pertained specifically to the new additions. With their knowledge and wisdom we puzzled through the logic and values of the most painful and difficult practical and philosophical judgments that had to be made.

 With passion akin to a religious zeal, ardent preservationists decried the project as an irresponsible act that trivialized the importance of Sage Hall – even of history itself. Theirs was a "sectarian," almost fundamentalist,

The Preservation Question

position admitting no discourse or disagreement, considering none but their own views as valid or worthy. Many of the strongest detractors shunned public meetings, participating in none of the open colloquy created by the civic processes that were followed assiduously; and then they claimed due process wasn't served.

Those who did contribute to the public discussion are real benefactors of a future for Sage Hall. We applaud and appreciate their "non-sectarian" engagement with the process. They are the true preservationists – preserving their values and integrity while participating creatively and constructively and, in the end, preserving the vision of Ezra Cornell and the values he espoused.

The preservation, reconstruction and expansion of Sage Hall has relied upon a few simple themes:

- Create a Business School of the twenty-first century.

- Preserve and enhance the original spirit and fabric of the place.

- Reconstruct Sage Hall in the footprint of the original.

- Design an expansion thematically inspired by the original but abstractly differentiated from it…to be clear about the timeline of history.

The Preservation Question

And, of course, Dean Merton's exhortation to dazzle him!

The District Court dismissed the Heritage Foundation's case that the Ithaca city boards with oversight had acted improperly when they granted a building permit for Sage the previous March, but the Heritage Coalition went on to appeal to the State Supreme Court, extending the uncertainty of the project's future. Other issues also created public concerns. Eric Dicke alerted members of the project team, via e-mail, to problems with the public's perceptions regarding the asbestos removal that was one of the earliest phases of the renovation.

4/1/96
From: Eric Dicke [*responding to a draft press release that mentioned the upcoming asbestos removal*]

It may be a detail (though not perceived as one), but we will not begin asbestos removal until after the building is vacated, May 15. We will be doing some wall underpinning, site utility work, and the exterior wall supports (that you mentioned). Thx, Eric

[*Eric is right. The asbestos detail is important. People will flip out if they think the activities starting early are asbestos removal. Bob*]

Public perception was an ongoing strategic challenge to the team; in addition, there was the general inconvenience of working in an occupied building on a busy campus. Bob began to mentally prepare those who would be impacted by what he knew would be a long and difficult process.

The Preservation Question

4/1/96
From: Bob

To: Occupants of Sage Hall

This is NOT an April Fools Joke! This is really happening!

Hi folks:

Nice to meet you via the phone today. Hope to have a face to face (no face-offs please) soon. Well, the fur is flying as you've noticed. Being project manager, I knew enough to be out of town last week when Paul Sarokwash [*asbestos removal project manager*] and Sharon Wargo went out to post notices about the closing of the "D" lot. Seriously, it was a trip scheduled before I even got this assignment. From now on, I'm on the job and on campus.

The most pressing immediate concern seems to be deliveries to the courtyard. These should take place just like they normally do.

Another concern is pedestrian access to the building. All entrances except the south entrance next to the Henry [*a large room on the south side of the building*] and the tunnel will stay open. There will be gates in the construction fence for this purpose.

The Henry will be a noisy place at times. There will be excavation going on outside the window. We may need to block off part (half?) of the room at a time to keep you safe. If you know of scheduled events in that room, please let me know who, what, when and how long. We'll figure out how to work around each other.

There are two things I want you to remember.

The Preservation Question

1) We have to get through this until you're permanently relocated. We'll make this as painless as possible, but it will be painful at times. Call me whenever you need to.

2) Angela Mesmer has a bottle of TUMS.

Allan Lentini is arranging a meeting for Friday so we can start to talk this out. Stay tuned!

Regards, Bob

Allan had been leading what was called the "Sage Shuffle" for months, as the Grad School was moved to Caldwell Hall, and residents of Sage Hall were relocated to new lodgings in anticipation of the project. More tensions were revealed in subsequent messages chronicling the logistical problems of working around an academic schedule, and the uncertainties of the building site.

4/26/96
From: Bob

To the Cornell project team: Hal Craft, [*Vice President for Facilities and Campus Services*], Steve Wright, Eric Dicke, John McKeown [*director of business operations for the Business School*], and Bob Libby [*who had chastised Bob S. for spending contingency funds to keep the work going off hours*]

Gentlemen:

Last night (about 5pm) we poured the first two (of 53) piers for the underpinning. The work was witnessed by Beacon, Haley and Aldrich, myself, and a technician from Empire Soils. Empire observed the mix

The Preservation Question

being prepared at the plant (Saunders), followed the truck to the site and collected test cylinders. Schnabel Foundation Company exposed the bedrock at the expected depth. One pier was poured on a very flat surface. The other was poured on a very irregular and split surface after H&A inspected and approved the condition.

As you know this is part of the scope of work at the southwest corner of the building accomplished on a second shift from 3pm to 11:30pm [*avoiding conflicts with classes*]. They will work this evening, possibly tomorrow and anticipate pouring again Monday evening. I have talked to the occupants and various students being tutored while the noisiest work is going on. They find it pretty obnoxious, but are toughing it out.

I'll use this format to notify you of significant events and will start to distribute weekly summary reports today. Let me know if there is more you would like to know about. Are there others you think should be included in the distribution?

Bob

Bob's optimism shines through in his reports to the community chronicling the progress of the Sage reconstruction. But he has also benefited from the Leadership Development Program at Cornell, which was originated by Hal Craft and now has spread to the rest of the University. This training served him well at Sage Hall in helping him to "lead others to successful outcomes through enhanced communication," reflecting the program's mission. Bob began to distribute his project updates to

The Preservation Question

the university's administrators, the contractors, JGSM and eventually the wider Cornell community.

Update 1
4/26/96

Good afternoon from the muddy front lines of the Sage Hall project. This is the first of a weekly news summary of what's happening. I would like to turn the less sensitive newsworthy items into a web site with photos. So far, there is only one page with a view of the finished building, but I want to fulfill the promise of more to come.

We have a contract! Bob Eckstein [*Beacon's Vice President and Project Executive*] returned to Boston with a signed copy of the agreement. Next week we'll process the first requisition. A paltry $300K compared to the average of $1M/mo from now until JGSM occupies in May '98.

Beacon Construction Company has set up offices on the second floor of Sage. It's pretty rag-tag, but these guys have seen rough conditions before. Hey, we've given them phones, chairs and tables, running water, and the roof doesn't leak. Heck, they've even had heat most days! Seems the occupants thought the heat was off because of the project and Beacon thought it was just a very inadequate system so no one called Customer Service to report a maintenance problem.

Beacon has worked hard at being good neighbors to the occupants. Paul Sarokwash and I have also kept in close contact with the occupants so that we can identify problem situations and keep them from getting out of hand. The asbestos containing plaster almost became that kind of situation.

The Preservation Question

Alan Lentini invited us to a meeting with the occupants to discuss the construction activities taking place around the building. Beacon made a presentation of the work and left. Paul and I stayed on to see if there was assistance we could render as people moved out. We realized that removal of items attached to the walls could disturb the plaster and pointed out that this could only be done by asbestos workers.

Some occupants became concerned (even angry) that they had been exposed to asbestos. We called a public information meeting for the occupants to discuss the nature of the extremely low risks for harm due to the plaster. Representatives from Environmental Health and Safety and the Galson Corporation (project asbestos consultant) reassured the occupants that they had not been unduly exposed to asbestos by their residence in Sage.

Beacon and I met with the City code enforcement officials to discuss expectations for required inspections. They were reassured by the list of the contractors that Beacon will use on the project and the commitment to perform quality work.

We've had several coordination meetings with the asbestos contractor, the movers, our utilities representatives and the Grounds Department. Very good cooperation from all concerned.

Grounds will soon relocate the beautiful white fir at the southeast corner of the building. This is a donor tree and the second time it has had to be relocated. I believe it was previously moved by the Statler project. Looks like this tree is something of a major facility divining rod. Maybe we should get Trustee approval before selecting the next site! We will get donor approval.

The Preservation Question

As you know, we're working the second shift (3-11:30pm) until May 4th to avoid conflicts with most, but not all of the classes in Sage. Last night we poured the first two (of 53) piers to underpin the exterior walls that we will salvage. Next pour should be Tuesday evening.

Weather has produced some sloppy conditions on the site. If you visit, you'll need appropriate foot wear as well as a hard hat. If you don't have a hard hat, Beacon can accommodate visitors. If you expect to visit regularly, I can provide you with your own. (John McK, yours is rattling around my car, acquiring a well-worn patina so the contractors will think you're an old hand at this stuff!) Let me know if you'd like a tour.

Look ahead activities: Utility relocations, provisions for Beacon offices in trailers, more underpinning, occupants continue to move out.

Stay tuned,

Bob

    Cornell has a rich history of student activism when the weather warms up in the spring, and a demonstration forced the closure of East Avenue one afternoon as the Sage construction crew was ready to leave. People at the university tend to view the disruption as part of the local color, but for the building tradespeople it was another reminder of the special problems created by working on a college campus. While addressing incidental concerns, Bob set out the "partnering agreement" he had worked out with the various players on his team in his next update,

The Preservation Question

in line with his mission to prioritize full partnership and clear communication within the group.

Update 2
5/10/96

Rain continues to be a nuisance for the contractors on site. April was the fifth wettest since 1879. Well, it keeps the dust down!

Thursday, General Arborists relocated the white fir on the southeast of Sage to the island between Barton and Statler. They took special care with the tree as it was donated by their deceased boss, John Eunicki. The tree looks great in its new home [*sadly, it later had to be moved again, when the School of Hotel Administration expanded for the Beck Center, and subsequently died*].

Poangeli Construction has started excavating for major utility relocations along the south side of the site. Things got a little tense Thursday night when Pogo's troops weren't able to go home because of the [*vehicular disruption caused by the*] protest. He claimed that his folks were demanding overtime compensation and that "someone would have to pay." Lucky for Pogo he had an experienced project manager (Hal Craft) on hand to calm him down somewhat at which point a CU Police bike officer (Officer Cole) appeared by coincidence. Pogo's two or three trucks wanted to get out of the area and the officer offered to lead them out by way of the sidewalk on Tower Road past the ILR project. Pogo agreed and off they all went. I was stuck in traffic so my thanks to Hal and Officer Cole!

Schnabel Foundation will cease evening shift work on the underpinning this week. Back to daylight hours for the mole people!

The Preservation Question

Tuesday, we spent the day drafting a partnering agreement for the project management team for The Hillier Group, JGSM, Facilities and Contract Services, and Beacon.

In summary:

> We pledge to work together as a team in an open communications climate to ensure a successful project for all. We want to accomplish the project in a financially responsible way. We will take the necessary time to clearly communicate what we need and when, and understand the context of the request with other priorities. Our immediate priorities are to achieve the value engineering goals for quality and cost and to take advantage of the project schedule to achieve exceptional coordination between the various trades.

Cornell Dining served their last meal in Sage Friday afternoon. They began moving out Saturday.

The remaining occupants are also moving out over the next two weeks.

Look ahead activities: Underpinning will begin on the northeast part of the building. University Counsel submits our papers May 6th in the ongoing legal fight over the City of Ithaca's approval process with the Heritage Coalition.

Stay tuned for the remaining 50 episodes of "The Sage Hall Renovation."

Bob

Despite the court-ordered injunction against working on the exterior of the historic building, the team was moving forward with

The Preservation Question

preparations for the asbestos removal, the necessary first step for the renovation. Although <5% of the interior plaster walls had <5% of asbestos in samples, every bit of it was handled as hazardous material because the asbestos was distributed randomly.

Update 3
5/28/96

Better (mostly) weather finally arrives. Well, for construction at least.

It was a wild week as the last occupants moved out, the asbestos contractor [*LVI Services*] moved in, we disconnected utilities, made provisions for temporary power and water, moved Beacon to the Grad student office, and conducted various salvage operations.

Many of LVI's workers are Polish immigrants so we have Polish/English safety signs posted. They are very hard working individuals. Paul Sarokwash made arrangements for LVI to rent rooms in one of the frat houses. Very beneficial arrangement for all concerned. The cook gets to work the summer, the house earns some extra money, and the workers don't have to hassle with parking (they walk to Sage).

Underpinning is proceeding. We have some constraints because of the need to avoid disturbing the historic exterior [*because of the ongoing lawsuit*]. This is mainly a problem around the entrances, but so far we have figured reasonable work-arounds.

Caisson drilling will start next month. The rebar has already been fabricated on site. The caissons become the foundation upon which the wall retention system will be erected.

The Preservation Question

Poangeli is continuing its site utility work. The Utilities Department took advantage of this to replace a short section of sanitary waste line.

Beacon's trailer office complex is taking shape. A single unit that will be mated to a double wide was delivered this week.

Bob

    Steve Sharratt, Executive Director of Development and Assistant Dean for External Relations for the Johnson School (who would go on to become director of operations for the Parker Center for Investment Research at JGSM), enlisted Bob to help give tours of the building, especially to alumni who might be potential contributors to the project.

6/10/96
From: Steve Sharratt

Bob:

Thanks so much for leading the tour of Sage Hall on a hot Saturday afternoon. Our alumni really enjoyed and appreciated your presentation. One couple wrote a check out on the spot, and your eloquence is inspiring other plans for naming gifts (the Class of '76 is – seriously – planning to raise money for a "Gross Bob McConnell" Room; I wonder what the committee on memorials will make of that?).

Thanks again!

Steve Sharratt

The Preservation Question

[*This is the kind of feedback I really like to hear. We shook the money tree and something fell out! Bob*]

The Heritage Coalition appealed the State Supreme Court's decision in March to let the Sage Hall project go forward. The University asked the Appellate Division for an expedited ruling, since they were already proceeding with interior work on the building while complying with the injunction. In June, the Appellate Court turned the Heritage Coalition down again, as reported in the *Cornell Chronicle*:

6/20/96
Court Rules Sage Work Can Proceed, by David Stewart

> Exterior work on historic Sage Hall may now proceed without restraint, thanks to a unanimous decision by the Appellate Division of Third Department of the New York State Supreme Court on June 14.
>
> The Heritage Coalition Inc. of Syracuse, a preservation group, and local resident Barbara Ebert had argued that two of Ithaca city boards – the Landmarks Preservation Commission and the Planning and Development Board – acted improperly when they granted Cornell permission to renovate and save the 123-year-old Sage Hall from deterioration. Sage is to become the new home of the university's S.C. Johnson Graduate School of Management.

The Preservation Question

It must meet strict standards for renovation because it was declared a local landmark in 1990.

The appellate ruling upholds a lower-court decision in March by State Supreme Court Justice Philip Rumsey, who dismissed the suit for "lack of standing" by either the coalition or Ebert.

"The Supreme Court's opinion added that, even if the petitioners had standing, neither city board had acted improperly," said Shirley K. Egan, associate university counsel, who represented Cornell in the case.

Both Ebert and the coalition appealed the Rumsey decision and requested a preliminary injunction pending appeal. The preliminary injunction, granted April 10, halted exterior work on Sage Hall until the appellate division could issue its ruling in the case. The university's motion for an expedited appeal was granted, and written arguments from the petitioners, the city and the university were submitted in late April and early May.

The case was heard on June 4, with Egan arguing on behalf of the university. In a three-page ruling, the appellate division unanimously affirmed the lower court's ruling that

The Preservation Question

the Heritage Coalition and Ebert did not have legal standing to bring the action.

Preliminary site work and asbestos removal were not affected by the injunction and have proceeded. Exterior work is slated to begin later this month, and construction is scheduled for completion in summer 1998.

But in fact, the Heritage Coalition made a final attempt to appeal the decision, again throwing a shadow of doubt over the project, and Bob's frustration is apparent in his next communiqué:

Update 4
6/24/96

Like the Terminator, The Heritage Coalition just won't take no for an answer. A week ago, we went home for the weekend knowing that they had lost their appeal to the Supreme Court Appellate Division. That also lifted the injunction. On Monday, we immediately began work on some steps and an areaway at the Head House (southeast corner) to enable us to continue underpinning. Because the decision was unanimous, they must get permission to appeal to the State's highest court, The Court of Appeals. That's what we learned they were doing Friday. We all know the Terminator was eventually defeated, but the plot kept us on the edge of our seats.

Well, we're not even in our seats at Sage. We're accelerating the asbestos removal and planning how to create a *fait accompli* while our hands are still untied. Can't do much until the asbestos is gone though, so that's the focus.

The Preservation Question

Speaking of seats, JG Furniture was the desired vendor for auditorium seating, but they were attempting to force us into an unacceptable deal: Pay 90% of the bid price now for seats we won't need until 3/98, or suffer a $100K price increase. Cornell's Purchasing Department did an excellent job of providing us with enough information about JG and alternative vendors (thanks to Hillier too) that Beacon was able to get JG to back off from their outrageous proposal. We're back to a normal arrangement and we have options if we smell a rat [*Bob's instincts were turned out to be correct, as JG filed for Chapter 7 bankruptcy in April of 1998, just before shipping the chairs*].

The caisson-drilling rig finally arrived along with the rain. Sometimes it looks like they're drilling wells. The first rig was a little undersized for the task of drilling 4 feet into the bedrock, but a meatier rig arrived on Thursday so Beacon is getting into position to start erecting bracing steel on July 8th.

I went into the asbestos containment last week to get a feel for how the work was progressing and to inspect for structural unforeseens. The removal is moving along, but as I mentioned earlier, we've asked LVI to step it up. I only saw two areas where leaking roofs have rotted mansard roof structure. That will not be demolished so these areas must be repaired. Those of you who have walked around Sage know it's big and how convoluted the room layout is. We have the whole northside of the building under removal. It's a lot of work.

The construction fence was moved around a little to accommodate the caisson rigs and dress things up a bit. Still need to do a little more to discourage pedestrians walking in the road along East Avenue.

The Preservation Question

Our neighbors seem to be tolerating our work for the most part. The weather has caused muddy conditions and quite a bit is traveling off-site. Beacon will improve soil retention and hire a service to clean the streets more frequently. Weekly isn't enough.

The project trailers should be ready to occupy on the 1st of July. Sharon Wargo and I will stay in 150 Baker Lab for the summer at least. Then I'll move on site to Sage while Sharon closes out Baker/Olin until the end of '96. Well, that's all for now, I'll let you know as soon as I hear anything on further legal developments.

Bob

Partly because of the wider distribution of Bob's progress reports, the asbestos removal attracted attention, reflected in an inquiry from an alumnus concerned about the Polish workers. The writer was a graduate of the Johnson School who would subsequently serve as Deputy Associate Administrator at the U.S. Environmental Protection Agency.

7/8/96

From: Donna Spinella [*Director of Alumni & International Relations for the Johnson School*]

Bob,

I got the following e-mail from one of our alums after forwarding your Sage update. I can respond if you give me information.

> I had heard that less than scrupulous NYC firms were using foreign nationals to remove asbestos in the NYC area – because the workers would do the work, didn't understand the risks, and would be unlikely to sue for physical harm 20

The Preservation Question

years from now (long after they had returned home). The working conditions violated OSHA/EPA rules. I trust LVI is adhering to the letter and spirit of sound worker protection and that Cornell has provisions in all its contracts for Sage that require contractors to be in full compliance with all applicable worker safety and environmental laws – including the disposal of any waste materials.   Why is the staff from Poland?

Rick Otis

Thanks, Donna

[*Donna: Thanks for passing along the inquiry from Rick Otis. His concerns are important to me and to the University so I will respond directly to him below. Bob*]

Dear Rick:

Sorry to trigger any alarm in you, but if I'd thought about it I would have guessed that others would have the same reaction I did when I learned about the Polish contingent.

I have been involved with asbestos removals at Cornell since 1980 and am one of the authors of our asbestos management plan. I supervise the Asbestos Project Coordinator, Paul Sarokwash, who is managing the asbestos portion of Sage. The health and safety of the Cornell community is very important to Paul and me, and we certainly include concern for the workers of any contractor on our campus.

I have also heard the same sorts of nightmares about NYC asbestos contractors that you refer to. I am confident that LVI is not that kind of contractor. All asbestos contractors working for Cornell are prequalified. LVI is a national firm and was recommended to us by our asbestos consultant as one of a select few reputable firms that

The Preservation Question

could perform the Sage Hall removals in accordance with our strict health and safety requirements.

Our asbestos consultant, Galson Corporation, is a nationally recognized environmental consulting firm. Galson designed the removal and provides continuous monitoring of the contractor to assure compliance with all relevant regulations. I have personally entered the work area unannounced and know that LVI is in compliance. According to Paul and Galson, and based on my own observations, LVI is performing at an above average standard for asbestos contractors at Cornell. The standard of performance at Cornell is much higher than for asbestos contractors in general.

We require any contractor working here to provide all applicable licensing for the firm and workers before they ever set foot on campus. Waste manifests are received for every load of asbestos disposed of (in licensed landfills). Extensive air monitoring is maintained throughout the removal to assure safety.

Why are many of LVI's workers from Poland? I don't know for certain, but I think it's because they are willing to work hard for above average hourly rates in a very unattractive job. They don't need extensive education or scholarly language skills. They just need to be willing to do it, and many people won't.

In summary: Cornell University has a sound asbestos management plan, we are a knowledgeable and demanding user of asbestos consulting and abatement services, and we are confident that our projects are conducted in as safe a manner as possible.

I hope I have addressed your concerns. Many people have the perception that our business schools turn out managers concerned only with the bottom line even at the expense of worker safety. It's

The Preservation Question

good to know that is not the case with graduates of JGSM. Thanks for caring. Please let me know if there is more you would like to know.

Regards,

Bob

From: Rick Otis

Bob,

Thanks. I suspected CU would be doing a good job with asbestos and assume the same goes for the general environmental aspects of the renovation job. Actually, corporate interest in constantly improving environmental performance and worker safety is not rare. Both have become an inherent part of business management today – often as crucial to the bottom line as any other business decision. The important role they play is generally not understood by the public. It is intentionally downplayed or lied about by politicians and their staff (including the current Administration in Washington and their Democratic colleagues on the Hill in order to impugn the motivations of the Republican Congress for partisan election purposes). You will see an increase in the number of companies building environmental considerations into their operations under such programs as ISO-14000 (an environmental version of the international quality manufacturing program called ISO-9000).

Indeed, our existing environmental laws may actually hinder continued environmental progress under such programs. Finally, academic business/environmental training programs often do not adequately incorporate such knowledge. Rensselaer Polytechnic's MBA program and Environmental Management Program do a very good job of incorporating corporate environmental performance as

The Preservation Question

an inherent and necessary part of business management. The program is run by Dr. Bruce Piasecki – a JGSM alum.

Good luck with Sage.

Rick

In his private communications, Bob the professional can give way to a more belligerent yet still witty Bob, when he feels free to vent. The project conditions were becoming more complex and less glamorous as the summer slogged on. For example, a drill rig on the East Avenue side of the building pierced the telecom duct bank, disrupting service to the Statler Hotel and the Cornell Campus Store...

7/15/96
From: Bob Stundtner
To: Eric Dicke

Eric:

Boy, did you pick a good time to be out of town. Hot, muggy, rainy... ugh! I wore black slacks today and they are mud to the knees. I showed up for our meeting this morning, but you were nowhere to be found. Sue Hartman [*one of Eric's staff members*] reminded me or I'd still be there fuming!

The second US Fence rig left without ever drilling a hole. The Cook rig is back together, but still not working. The crane is working, but they sent the guys home due to rain. Steel workers are so delicate.

Roger McCoy from LeMessurier [*structural engineering firm who designed the wall retention system*] is here and Robert Santiago of

The Preservation Question

Robert Silman Associates [*Hillier's structural sub-consultant*] was supposed to be here, but the flight was canceled. He'll be here about 5pm. They are meeting to check out the exposed structure in abated areas. Eckstein scheduled this without my knowledge. I told him I'd drag him around the site by his tongue (with whatever piece of equipment was working at the time) the next time he schedules a meeting before talking to me. Bonne and I had the same discussion as I just learned this morning she and Charlie [*from the Hillier Group*] are on their way Wednesday. Somehow, they all think I just sit here waiting for them to remember to invite me at the last minute. You been talking to them? Anyway, I'm going to have to kick butt if they don't cut it out. They are too used to working without much owner participation in construction. As Tricky Dick said, "I have a plan!"

It was raining inside the building harder than it was outside this morning. Go figure. Definitely no swimming pool under the 1894 addition. Somebody took a dump at the top of the stairs. Joe thinks it's a dog. Right, a 250lb dog! The water acquires a brownish tone as it seeps down through the building. New rule: don't look up with your mouth open.

Jeff Wilbur called. Those were 2200 & 2400 pr NYNEX cables, plus ours, plus Time Warner. We'll meet tomorrow to figure out how to fix and stay out of more drilling.

Bob Whitty, Pres CFCU called Hal late Thurs. All of Bailey Hall branch and Campus Store ATM were still off line. Pay day, of course! I calmed him down, briefed Hal and Friday Sharon got Telecom to get them back up by 10:30am. He's assembling his claim and I told him we'd make sure it was resolved.

The Preservation Question

Check the docs I sent to Keith Boncek [*IT person for Facilities Services*]. JGSM wants to go fiber to the desk! I'll tell you THG, Acentech [*Hillier's A/V subconsultant*], and ESA [*Hillier's teledata subconsultant*] did not put on a stellar performance at that meeting last week. We should talk about this some more.

Learning anything useful? Hope the food is good. DC is no place to have rubber chicken, but I guess it comes with the conference at only a small extra charge. Enjoy!

Bob

> The project team had problems keeping people out of the work site in one of the busiest parts of campus, mostly people who were merely resistant to changing their walking habits.

8/1/96
From: Bob
To: David Stewart [*Director of Community Relations*]

David:

We're having some difficulty with pedestrians walking in the road along East Avenue from the bus shelter to Wee Stinky Glen [*a small green area with a creek running through it between Sage and Day Hall*]. We already have several trucks pulling in and out of the site gate on East Avenue daily. Wait 'til we really pick up a head of steam! Any ideas on how we could publicize this problem and warn the community about the risk? We have signs up all over, but some people seem to ignore them. Any thoughts you may have would be greatly appreciated.

Regards, Bob

The Preservation Question

[Bob: Two thoughts. One, arrest them.

Two, you could send a short "letter-to-the-editor" of the Chronicle, *combining your concern and humor. The* Chronicle *would need such by end of the day Friday (8/2). Maybe the* Chronicle *editor (Simeon Moss) could assign a photographer to get a shot of what's on the signs, etc. You could also send the same letter to the* Daily Sun *for use in late August.*

Yet another idea. Why not close the walkway further back from the actual site? David I. Stewart]

A more exotic security issue arose in the form of a late night student prank, as Claude Leblanc, Beacon's General Superintendent, informed Bob in an e-mail of September 5th:

Intruder Alert!

Bob,

I received a phone call from the Cornell Police at 2:30 a.m. last evening. Apparently they received a complaint from someone at the Statler that there was noise coming from the site. They sent someone over and found a student, who had hopped the fence, was on site and was inebriated. He claimed that he only wanted to climb onto the crane. Sgt. Kathy Kowler told me that there were two options;

1. Press for criminal trespassing charge.

2. Cornell has a judicial board that he would have to appear before. I asked if the person had been injured, and was told no. I asked if there was any damage and they said not that they could determine.

The Preservation Question

Given these facts, I told the Sgt. that I did not believe that we would want to press charges, but that I would check in the a.m. to see if there was any damage. She stated that the student (a senior), was quite shaken by the fact that he could be facing criminal charges. I checked with Brownell (crane owner) and outside of an empty beer bottle, did not find anything out of order.

Claude

[*What's Next?*

Well, you can bet we'll be conducting a risk evaluation of the surrounding area including traffic flow, pedestrian circulation and especially site security!

For the next few weeks the project is in its most exciting and nerve wracking phase as selective removal proceeds. However, there's an enormous and much less glamorous effort that takes place out of public view. More on what it is we do all day in my next update. Bob]

The summer of 1996 had been challenging for me as well, in different ways. My short and troubled relationship with a French glassblower had ended badly (although definitely for the best, and my son Patrick was glad to see him go). Pat and I spent the third weekend of July at the Finger Lakes Grassroots Festival in Trumansburg, the annual local musical gathering with a national reputation for its roots music and mellow ambiance. I had helped to launch the event in 1990 by recruiting the former Highwoods Stringband members to reunite for the festival, which drew people from as far away as the Midwest that first year. By 1996, the

The Preservation Question

festival was well into its established routine, featuring African, Cajun and Zydeco, and local world-beat artists from our talented local music scene.

The week after the festival, Patrick left Ithaca to spend the rest of his summer vacation in Pennsylvania with my parents. Alone in my little condominium on East Hill, I contemplated the future, focusing on Pat's and my own well-being, and how best to work towards that goal. Watching the morning news one day, I saw the wonderful Irish vocalist Mary Black performing outdoors in Dublin, singing "straight out of the blue, all in one sweet instant, the summer sent you." It moved me; I found the CD downtown and pondered the mysteries of love through Mary's interpretations of Celtic songs.

That weekend, knowing that music would help to lift my spirits, I decided to go down the hill to Micawber's Pub for the bar's Sunday evening Irish session for the first time. It's a favorite bar of the townies for happy hour and the college students for late night drinks. Inevitably in what locals fondly call our "Tiny Town," I knew some of the musicians, who invited me to come back the next weekend with my flute and whistles. Subsequently I joined them for five o'clock happy hours at the bar on Fridays.

Bob was recently single as well. He knew the musicians who formed the core of the Irish session, and was sitting at the

The Preservation Question

opposite end of the bar the first night I showed up at Micawber's. Each of us was alone, just as we had been at the Grassroots Festival the weekend before, hearing the same music but hearing it separately. We were introduced the next Friday at happy hour, and I noticed his jacket and tie among the generally more casual crowd. Bob was well liked by the other men, and respected as a longtime Cornell stalwart. He would leave early to care for his dog, Cilantro, adopted from the local Farmer's Market.

I guess Bob noticed me too, and unexpectedly love entered our lives. After the Irish session the next Sunday, he came over and sat with me as I put my instruments away. As we chatted he mentioned that he had been going to Negril, Jamaica for vacations since the 1980's, and that he was going to retire there. "Jamaica?" I said wide-eyed, "I've never been to the Caribbean." Bob said later that we warped space and time to be together, but in retrospect it looks like he had planned it all out; after all, "prior proper planning prevents poor performance," something every project manager knows. Bob credits the endorphins of new love with helping him deal with the stress of the renovation of Sage Hall, although we didn't start dating until October. And the tension around the project was mounting, as the legal challenge was still unresolved at the end of July.

Update 5
8/5/96

The Preservation Question

It's been awhile since I last distributed this news e-mail so you might suspect that nothing has happened or that I've been slacking off. Mea culpa, mea culpa – I've been slacking off! It is the best time of year to do that, but I promise to be more regular.

Beacon and many of the subcontractors on the site are beginning to believe that the Heritage Coalition has resorted to slapping a hex on us in lieu of an injunction. We have suffered a series of equipment breakdowns that seem to be more than our fair share. For a brief period we had three drilling rigs and a crane broken down on the site. They all broke down just after a telecom duct bank was accidentally damaged and several NYNEX customers lost service for up to two days. The construction industry understands Murphy's Law better than most, but most of July was too much.

As for the status of the Heritage Coalition, no news is good news. However we sure would like to know that the Court of Appeals has denied their request for permission to appeal.

The asbestos contractor, LVI, has completed the second phase of the asbestos removal and has started the last. Overall, they are slipping in their schedule by perhaps two weeks, but impact on the project should be nominal. It is very hard to sustain production on large asbestos projects like this where workers are doing the same thing for two shifts day in and day out. LVI has rotated their people to reduce this impact, but they seem to be running on a bit less steam lately.

As soon as LVI finishes each phase, we go in to inspect. The exposed brick and stonewalls and wood frame structures are very interesting. We all marvel at the details of the original construction and myriad renovations that Sage has undergone. Some of the renovations resulted in downright wacky structural changes. It's a good thing

The Preservation Question

buildings are stronger than the sum of their parts. If you've ever renovated an old house, you probably know what I'm talking about.

Various unforeseen conditions are being uncovered as we go in to inspect the abated areas of Sage. The north wing has some dry rot in the mansard roof valleys, but the west wing seems to be relatively free of the problem.

The advent of electricity and especially the upgrade from knob and tube distribution to metal jacketed cable caused the most damage to the building. New circuits were added to masonry walls by chopping holes and channels in the brick. Where this has weakened the structural integrity of walls to be reused, we have to make repairs. To date our total exposure for these unforeseens is not excessive.

No, that's not an addition being added on the north and east side of the building. Those are the steel towers for the retention system that will hold up the exterior walls while the selective removals are underway and until the walls are tied into the new structure.

Rain continues to be a mixed blessing. It keeps the dust down, but that clay sure is sticky and slippery when wet. The street sweeper does a great job, but a couple of trucks leaving the site can undo his best efforts pretty quickly.

The mechanical, electrical and plumbing contractors are still working with the various consultants to fit all of the equipment into the ceilings. This is proving to be hard, but progress is being made and we expect the necessary coordination with the structural steel to be achieved.

The Hillier Group and Cornell Information Technologies are working with JGSM to review and update the audio/visual and voice/data

The Preservation Question

design. At the moment we have a greater than two year lag between the design and installation. That's a lifetime in those fields and we want to maximize the purchasing power of our tight budget.

Transportation Services and CU Police are collaborating with Beacon to devise a safe and efficient delivery plan for the site. Selective removal and basement excavation will require hundreds of truckloads of debris and soil to be removed from the site. The delivery of new structural steel and the pouring of concrete floor slabs will also require many deliveries in a brief period of time. Sage is located on the corner of what may be the busiest intersection on campus. Timing deliveries for the brief gaps between class changes, buses, and rush hour traffic will be a challenge that will make working the midnight shift sound attractive. Hmmm, the guests at the Statler might not like that.

Well, there's nothing easy about this project so I guess we'll just have to rise up to the challenge and be our best. Be writing you sooner,

Bob

[*From: Shirley K. Egan [Associate University Counsel]*

Bob – Many thanks for the enlightening and entertaining update. You have an alternative career as a writer if you'd like! I know you're anxious for the court to turn down the appeal attempt, but I'd feel better if you had the kitchen wing in dump trucks before the decision came out. I can't guarantee they'll nix the application for leave to appeal, so the safest bet is to use the time to engineer a fait accompli. I'm disheartened to learn about all the little setbacks at the site since I sense they are what's keeping you from doing that. Keep me posted! Shirley]

The Preservation Question

[Hi, Shirley. Thought I might hear from you. I'd like to give you a tour of the building because I think you might credibly argue that we have the *fait accompli* already. Besides, it's enormously interesting to get a peek inside. What do you say? If you have time tomorrow, I'll take you on a tour. Just wear VERY sensible shoes. Tell me when and I'll pick you up. Bob]

The next project update was dramatic, as one of the walls inside the building began to move. The brick wall was on the south side of the interior courtyard, where the atrium joins the dining area now, part of the troubled history of Sage Hall that was revealed during the renovation. The original dining area had wooden trusses that failed a century ago, that had first been patched together with 1½" steel rods; then, in the 1920's or '30's, brick buttresses were built to reinforce the original structure. Bob thinks that by the time the asbestos contractors were removing it, the plaster was the only thing holding the mansard roof to the wall.

The asbestos crew had been working for two months without a break, in two shifts, seven days a week, removing the plaster and piling it in the center of the building. It was the Monday after their first weekend off when the wall started to move above a second floor window. When it was noticed, Bob ran up to the third floor and could see a gap between the floor and the exterior wall. He grabbed some wood lath and placed it on the floor to measure the movement; later, he found that it had moved 18" in the course of the day. Bob remembers that when he saw

The Preservation Question

that, he got out quickly and quietly...as he told an *Ithaca Journal* reporter with some understatement, "The wall was just kind of going out on its own..."

Update 6
8/15/96

Well, so much for the promised regularity to these updates. This week gave new meaning to unforeseen conditions.

As most of you know, about 70 feet of the courtyard wall of the south wing has a very impressive bulge in it at the top of the brick where it meets the mansard roof. The wall is out about 18 inches at its extreme. In the course of Monday morning, the wall moved several inches. Since then, it has moved an additional inch. Additional surveys have confirmed no movement in the south wall of this wing that will remain for the restoration.

This was reported at 7am on Monday morning by the asbestos contractor. Although only 3 days from being completely done, all asbestos removal in the south wing was halted.

Gary Kochinsky [*a structural engineer*] of our own Planning, Design, and Construction Department gave us our first piece of advice. "Get out!" Gary was shocked at how poorly designed, constructed, repaired and currently unstable this part of the building was.

Although not their work area, Beacon Construction was very cooperative in marshaling problem solving resources. On Tuesday, we convened a daylong session to investigate and develop a plan to stabilize the structural stresses without damaging the south wall and most importantly not putting workers at undue risk.

The Preservation Question

Attendees included Bob Silman, Robert Silman Associates, structural consultant to The Hillier Group; Roger McCoy, LeMessiuer, structural consultant to Beacon for the retention system; Peter Nelson, Nelson Associates, structural consultant to Integrated Waste, Beacon's demolition subcontractor; Steve Crawford, Integrated's project manager; Bob Eckstein and Claude LeBlanc from Beacon; Ron Thorp, Galson Corp.; Paul Sarokwash, Eric Dicke and me.

All of the structural consultants agreed with Gary Kochinsky's analysis that the wing was poorly designed, constructed, and repaired. By the end of the day the team achieved a consensus on how to safely resolve the problem. The plan was to be put in place as soon as all the material and equipment was on site. Unfortunately, the wall continued to move Tuesday night and Integrated no longer felt the plan was safe.

A second round of problem solving focused on using heavy equipment to support the roof and remove the damaged portion of the wall before putting workers inside to brace up the roof. Posts were added on the first floor where they could be installed with minimal risk. Further, all work in the vicinity of this wing has been halted as a precautionary measure.

Friday we expect delivery of a second grapple rig and we plan to accomplish the removal and shoring on Saturday. Monday, we evaluate what additional steps must be taken to allow completion of the asbestos removal.

Elsewhere on the project, steel erection for the bracing system is proceeding on the west side and the new tunnel is past the first

Ed's Heads, casualty of the "Voodoo Wall" collapse
Photo by Robert P. Stundtner

The Preservation Question

stages of its construction. The coordination of the mechanical, plumbing and electric with the structural steel is still proving to be difficult, but the subs are working very hard to achieve it in time for the steel.

Special thanks to Ruben Rogers [*Director of Contracts Management*] and Patricia McClary [*Associate University Counsel*] for their assistance in creating the necessary contractual protection for all parties to deal with our wall problem.

And finally, I'm here to testify that guys that shave their heads can be harried. At least when the week is like this one!

Bob

Bob, with his smooth head, is known as Marblehead in Jamaica, and has often joked that he is chosen for the tough projects because he can't pull his hair out! The risks associated with the wall were great. Hal Craft convened Steve Wright, Ruben Rogers, Pat McClary, Eric Dicke and Bob for a final review of the plan to deal with the wall. A false move would bring it down on the opposite side of the building, which was intended to be salvaged. Bob told them that he would observe the contractors' interior bracing installation, a necessary first step in demolishing the bulging wall safely. He felt that it was important to verify that the workers were adhering to the engineered bracing plan. The attorneys, Ruben and Pat, protested that Bob ran the risk of impinging on the contractors' "means and methods," thereby muddying responsibilities if things went wrong, and potentially

The Preservation Question

risking his own safety. Bob assured them that he could observe safely from a structurally sound, adjacent stair well. Hal concluded the discussion by stating that he trusted Bob's judgment in the matter. It remains Bob's most treasured vote of confidence.

An e-mail message from Hal Craft reflects the seriousness with which the University was taking the challenges of the Sage project, and also the building's status as a major new landmark on campus.

8/22/1996
From: Hal Craft

Bob – Would you consider putting Hunter [*Rawlings, President of Cornell*] (via Ann Huntzinger), Don Randel [*University Provost*], Fred Rogers [*Senior Vice President of Cornell*], and Hank Dullea on your distribution list? Would this change the very delightful style and tone of your updates? They're great – informative, but with humor.

On a separate matter, would it be useful or appropriate to try to take Hunter, Don and Fred through the building at some point so they get a first-hand sense of the project? I realize that there will be no building soon, so maybe this is a bad idea. At any rate, I'd like somehow to give our senior leaders a real sense for what is going on and the complexity of the job.

Hal

[*Hal: I think you're absolutely right about the importance of having a sense of what's going on and the complexity. It might save you from having to justify in detail every unforeseen bit of the contingency. Especially with Fred's facilities background the reaction might be,*

The Preservation Question

"Ouch! Could have been worse." Also, it's a very interesting project. Of course, that seems to be the norm on our campus.

I'd be glad to guide the tour (group or individual), but I think Eric should be there too. He's back Wednesday. We have a regularly scheduled meeting with Steve on Thursday and I suspect Steve will hold the meeting on site. Normal trade working hours are 7am-3:30pm. Eric and I are available for this tour any daylight hour. 30 minutes min/1 hr max. Deb Chilson (Eric's Administrative Assistant) has access to both our MtgMkr schedules. Bob]

Bob's reports continued to be distributed to Cornellians beyond the campus, as word of the scale of the project spread. For example, Donna Spinella forwarded the next update to CU alumni with this note:

> Following is another installment in the ongoing Sage saga, direct from the keyboard of project manager Bob Stundtner, who's a little bit of Dave Barry, Bob Villa, and Scotty ("Captain, she can't take much more, ah'm givin' her all that I've got,") rolled into one...

Update 7
9/21/96

Delayed Broadcast from the Sage Hall Asbestos Free Zone:

On Sunday August 25th, Sage Hall was declared asbestos free. Well, for the small, nominal removal cost of $1.5 million, it wasn't exactly free, was it? And to be precise, there is still some asbestos roof felts left under the slates that we did not remove. However, compared to the 2,250,000 pounds of asbestos debris removed by LVI

The Preservation Question

Environmental Services, we can think of the building as free of asbestos.

Congratulations to LVI, Galson Corporation, and Paul Sarokwash as the successful team of contractor, environmental consultant, and Cornell asbestos project manager for completing the University's largest single asbestos removal project safely, profitably, within budget and without adverse schedule implications for the overall project.

The brick curtain falls on the week of the Wall:

The voodoo wall finally met its match on Friday August 16th. All week long, the wall kept moving and unraveling our plans for safely dismantling it. Heavy equipment with a long extension claw was brought in for a planned Saturday lancing of the eye-popping bulge. However, severe thundershowers Thursday night caused another major movement that continued Friday morning. We scrambled to assemble the equipment and set 1pm for a little wall surgery.

Word spread of the impending effort to safely remove the bulge and a small crowd of onlookers gathered across the street at the Statler bus stop. We convened the project team for one last review of the plan. When everyone was assured we had in place what we needed to safely proceed, we went to work. The Integrated Waste Services equipment operator did a very precise job of reaching up and gently poking the center of the bulge. Like a giant soap bubble being poked, the wall flexed inward over a foot and then sprang back out onto the tines of the outreached claw. A few tense seconds passed and then the operator moved the claw upward a couple of inches. Just as we planned, the claw supported the roof and the bricks fell away in a crash of noise and dust.

The Preservation Question

We waited a few minutes to review how stable the roof and remaining wall were. Once we were confident conditions were safe to go inside, Integrated went in to brace up the walls and roof. By 3pm we were done and the only casualties were two Port-a-johns. Sarokwash had turned away Ed's Heads from servicing the two toilets, noting they hadn't been used all week. He had to sign a receipt acknowledging access was blocked, preventing servicing. One unit is about half as tall as it used to be and the other is full of bricks that are tumbling out the door. It's an image that inspires all the "brick" joke clichés.

Additional monitoring and a few more braces allowed the asbestos removal to proceed to its successful conclusion. Now, the wall retention system is nearing completion and Integrated is back working on their selective removal work. Stay tuned for their "planned" work. It should be just as interesting as the unforeseen voodoo wall effort.

Bob

[*From: Paul Sarokwash: Thanks for the honorable mentions. I think you missed your calling – you should have been a writer for soap opera series. This last episode was exciting, well written, and left me hungering for more. Can't wait 'til next week – or can I?*]

The legal challenges obstructing progress on the Sage Hall project were finally and happily resolved when the Court of Appeals denied the Heritage Coalition the right to appeal, as reported in the *Cornell Chronicle* of September 5th:

> Appeal of Sage Hall rulings denied: The New York State Court of Appeals last week rejected a petition by the

The Preservation Question

Heritage Coalition Inc. for permission to appeal lower court rulings on Cornell's Sage Hall building project... "People interested and knowledgeable about historic preservation were consulted from the earliest planning stages of this project. Much of their input was willingly incorporated into the design. Cornell's architects and historic preservation consultants developed a real win-win plan. Most people involved in historic preservation, such as the Ithaca Landmarks Preservation Commission and the community's local historic organization, Historic Ithaca Inc., recognized this and supported it. It's unfortunate there was a lawsuit at all, when there are needy historic preservation projects out there that could have used such resources," said Shirley Egan, associate university counsel.

Naturally, Bob was very relieved that the project could go forward as planned, and outlined the upcoming challenges of the renovation process in his next update.

Update 8
9/9/96

Heritage Coalition Denied!

On Thursday, August 29 Associate University Counsel, Shirley Egan received word from the Court of Appeals that in the matter of Heritage Coalition Inc., et al, appellants, v. City of Ithaca, et al, respondents, "Motion for leave to appeal denied." With those few

The Preservation Question

words, the threat of a court decision that would interrupt or even halt the project came to an end.

Johnson (Graduate School of Management), we have separation!

Earlier that day the first phase of separation began. This is a process to cut free the structure to be salvaged from that to be removed. It's an awesome sight to look up three stories and see the exterior wall and slate mansard roof standing free against the blue sky above.

Slowly and very, very carefully Integrated Waste will conduct the separation stage of the selective removal process by hand. Separation will proceed in three phases starting in the north wing of Sage, then progressing to the west wing and finally the south. We're projecting 300 truckloads of 60 or 100 cubic yards apiece. Once separation is complete, the large grapples will return to remove the bulk of the building. The south wing remains troublesome for us even though we've removed the voodoo bulge. Whether or not equipment can be used in that wing is currently the subject of a careful engineering and risk analysis. How do we work safely and efficiently without damaging the walls we want to retain? We have about a month to sort those choices out.

By this time, Bob and I were sitting at the same round corner table most Friday evenings at Micawber's, and within a month we would have our first date, but I didn't know it yet. I was busy teaching and parenting, very much a day-to-day proposition, and was oblivious to Bob's plans to ask me out. And I wasn't on the distribution list for his updates yet, but this is one of my favorites because it is so emblematic of Bob's dedication to his work, his team, and his university.

View from the roof of the Statler Hotel, September 27, 1996
© *Jon Reis Photography*

The Preservation Question

Update 9
9/21/96

I am the very model of a modern project manager! On a serious note... (no, really) just because I pen these irregular updates, don't get the impression that this is a one-man show. It's not. While Bob Dole and Hillary Clinton may debate whether it takes a family or a village, I'm here to tell you that when it comes to raising a project of this scale it takes a pretty big slice of the Cornell Community.

I always chuckle whenever I read or hear about what "Cornell" is doing. As if "Cornell" were some monolithic entity. The same is true of the Sage Hall project manager. While I have the privilege of saying "I'm the project manager," the reality is that I'm just one of many people involved in the management of this project.

For this update I want to focus on my colleagues in Facilities and Campus Services who are the "modern project managers." I have to start with my home office, Maintenance Management. The breadth and depth of project management responsibilities and the diversity of the staff has provided me a constantly renewing source of ideas and experience that has kept me challenged and growing for over sixteen years. Whatever success I have as a project manager I owe in large part to all of the people I've worked with in that office.

On a day-to-day basis, Paul Sarokwash, Sharon Wargo and Eric Dicke work very hard to help me keep my head above water. Paul is our field lieutenant attending to all sorts of site details on a daily basis. He was instrumental in launching the site work and managed the very successful asbestos removal.

Sharon's most important contribution is to lighten my load on the Baker/Olin project. She's also the requisition disciplinarian.

The Preservation Question

Contractors and consultants alike quickly learn the necessity of providing proper backup for expenses and checking their math if they want to be paid promptly.

Eric's long history of shepherding the project provides the vision and thoughtful supervision I need. His sense of humor helps to bring balance to the degree of difficulty and seriousness of the task at hand. In a pinch, he's also a cheerful gofer.

As project accountant, Joan Bordenet keeps track of all the dollars. Rumor has it she has one or two other accounts [*it was actually more than 100 at the time*] to keep track of, but she makes me think mine is the only one.

It's no secret that while Ruben Rogers is Director, Nancy Phelps "is" Contracts Management. Who hasn't felt guilty asking for a contract to be cranked out yesterday ("...just this once!") and when were you ever told "no way?" If it really must be done, it is.

Ruben is every project manager's strategic reserve. Mostly, he offers cautionary notes in the margins of our meeting minutes. But when it really gets difficult, you call his direct line, and he figures out how to defuse the bomb you're sitting on.

So many people in Planning, Design and Construction provide so much support to a project like Sage, it's almost necessary to print off the entire staff directory. Without Randy Lacey and Anthony Putrello [*PDC engineers*], we couldn't make smart value engineering decisions. Gary Kochinsky provided our first engineering analysis on the wall that recently threatened imminent collapse. Jim Finnigan is designing the relocation of a damaged telecommunications duct bank. Dave Burnett keeps utility locations clearly marked out. Pat McNally is providing expertise to contain muddy storm water runoff from the

The Preservation Question

site. Bruce Bush and Art Stern are plotting shops support for commissioning building systems and quality assurance. From Transportation Services and Cornell University Police, Mike Lammuka and Randy Hausner are assisting with parking and traffic flow. Keith Haselman and John Smith are the Environmental Health and Safety reps helping us to keep the site safe. Dennis Osika and Pete Salino provide support and advice on grounds related issues.

It's not possible to manage a major project without the robust communications support provided by the Customer Service Center. Well, I think you get the picture. It takes a lot of people to manage the Sage Hall project. Next time, I'll tell you about the other members of the Cornell Community providing support to the project.

And the H.M.S. Sage? Most of the enabling work is accomplished so it's full speed ahead with mass removals. The kitchen wing really is a wing flappin' in the breeze today. Over the next four weeks, we'll all come to understand and appreciate what the steel towers around the building are for. You won't believe your eyes.

Chapter 5: The Transformation of Sage

Like many others in Ithaca, I had read about the collapse of the brick wall at Sage Hall in the local newspaper, but sitting in Micawber's one afternoon I was surprised to learn that Bob was the project manager for the renovation. I had a vague idea that he was some sort of engineer, and had never heard of project management, though I've learned since that the job has been compared to conducting an orchestra, in that it consists of getting disparate groups of people to work together harmoniously. One Friday early in October, Bob surprised me again when he invited me to go to hear a classical Indian flute concert at Barnes Hall with him the next Wednesday. I took a deep breath and said yes, and when Bob called on Monday to confirm the date, I suggested, and he agreed, that we have dinner together before the show.

We ate Middle Eastern food in Collegetown and walked up to the concert through a campus in full fall foliage. When we got to Barnes, a group of people, many clothed in colorful Indian textiles, had lined up to enter the small building. It became clear that the hall was full and we wouldn't get in. Bob proposed that we get his set of universal access keys from his car, so that we could enter via the back door to the concert hall and sit on the back stairs to catch the show. But his keys weren't in his car! We decided to drive to his house on the south side of town and get the keys, and we got back in time to enjoy most of the music. The flutist that night, Hariprasad Chaurasia, remains a favorite of ours.

Thursday morning Bob called to say that he'd enjoyed our date, and invited me to his house for dinner on Saturday. On Friday afternoon we were in our places at the round corner table by the window in Micawber's with Art Stern, a coworker of Bob's and one of the few people in Ithaca who had known both of us before we got together. Art mentioned to Bob that a blues band, Big Daddy Kinsey and the Kinsey Report, was playing at Key West, a bar by the inlet, that evening. It sounded like Bob might go, so I called him later to say I could join them. Bob and I danced together for the first time that night, laughing at the band's name and the potential implications of it all.

Saturday was a revelation for me. I had seen Bob's house briefly at night, but arriving in the afternoon I wasn't prepared for the natural beauty of the property. Encompassing 2.5 acres on South Hill, the land has a steep rise from the street to the defunct railroad bed that marks the boundary near the top of the hill. A small creek with a few waterfalls runs through a narrow gorge on the property, one of the many feeder creeks that cut through the Devonian sedimentary rock and glacial till to reach the level of the lakes, gouged out in former river valleys by the glaciers.

The Transformation of Sage

That afternoon, Bob and I carried hors d'oeuvres up to the "picnic rock" by the falls, and enjoyed goat cheese, a baguette, and a bubbly rosé from Australia. We were favored with a beautiful day, auspicious and affirming. Dinner was a rack of lamb, followed by dancing by the fire. Bob's plan was coming together...

In fact our relationship developed steadily, and the following e-mails, sent sporadically over the last half of October, chronicle its trajectory. I hadn't used electronic mail before, so it took me some time (and some help from Patrick) to get used to the technology. The flirting tone of the messages belies the underlying questions of a new relationship and what that might mean for all of us.

Jenny: Bob, it seems you have got me hooked on-line; the fun zone now! Still, it doesn't quite measure up to face-to-face communication.

Bob: No, it doesn't. But if it isn't a perfect substitute, it is a useful tool.

Jenny: Do high-powered managerial types ever get coffee/lunch breaks? I plan to be on campus tomorrow, and we could have a cup together if you feel like it and have the time.

Bob: For you? I'd make time most any ol' time, but I don't have to this time 'cause I have the time so what time? After 9am that is. Lunch is good. I think the weather is turning to poopy or at least rain tomorrow. Let me know what's convenient or play it by ear. Looking forward to seeing you. Your e-"pal" B-O-B

Jenny: You keep making me wish I checked my e-mail more often, but I don't have it on my desk (it's on Patrick's computer, and he didn't get off it since after you called this afternoon until just now, when I convinced him he needed to do some homework) and I don't want to get neurotic about it... I saw that a study showed that managers can suffer from stress because of TOO MUCH information in this information age, so let me just say that I am looking forward to our lunch tomorrow, and the hard-hat tour as well, and if you read this before tonight, or not for that matter, I am thinking about you, and I appreciate the way you have kept in touch with me, and the invitation to be in touch with you.

We walked from campus to Collegetown, as the neighborhood adjacent to the university is called, a few weeks later on another pleasant fall day, and had lunch at a Vietnamese restaurant. I was beginning to learn a bit about Bob's service in the Navy during the Vietnam War, a defining time in his life that we commemorate every Veteran's Day. On the way back to work, we took a detour through the gorge behind Rhodes Hall, crossing the Eddy Dam footbridge, among others enjoying the moderate temperatures.

Later, Bob suggested a weekend trip:

Thanks for the stress reducing lunch and walk today. Got to take advantage of the weather every opportunity these days. Store up the nice days for the long gray winter. Dig up the memories for warmth on a cold day. Today will go deep in the locker for one of those sub-zero days!

I was reminding myself about alternatives to local dancing this weekend. Ever been to the Dinosaur Bar and Grill in Syracuse? Great

The Transformation of Sage

BBQ, Blues, and funky clientele. A mix of bikers, yuppies and families. Looks like this weekend we really could be dancing up a storm so just wanted to say it out loud and then maybe you'd keep it in mind too for a li'l dining/dancing adventure.

Better bang out Beacon's change order cover letter. Be talking to ya!

The Dinosaur BBQ is definitely worth the hour drive to Syracuse, but we stayed in Ithaca that weekend, and Bob invited Patrick and me to dinner at his house. I got another chance to experience Bob's excellent culinary and grilling skills, as previewed in his e-mail invitation:

Nothing like a fire to take the chill off on a wet autumn night. The dance floor is ready. CD's are loaded. Will the rain let up enough to grill pork tenderloin? Can he cook something besides meat if it doesn't? Only one way to find out...

And Bob got to experience an evening with a 13-year old boy. After dinner Patrick walked downtown to hear a band at an early show at a club that admitted teenagers, and began to realize the potential benefits of living close to the city center.

Bob had signed Patrick on to his computer the night before, and reached out to him electronically the next day, sending some jokes and (what I at least recognized as) attempts to connect. Childfree until then, Bob still had a good sense of how to communicate with young people:

Bob: Thanks for hangin' in there and joining us for dinner. Hope it wasn't too weird. Did you leave me any interesting bookmarks?

The Transformation of Sage

Hear you're taking a course on the Cold War. The really scary thing about that period of our history is that guys like Dan Quayle were the Cold Warriors running things. Still are for that matter, but check it out and see if you sleep better knowing who's in charge!

Regards, Marblehead

Patrick: Hey Marblehead, Got yer message & last night wasn't that bad. Me & mom got a good laugh out of those quotes, the concert I went 2 was a lot of fun. In my cold war class I'm gonna bring in "Dr. Strangelove" cause it's on tonight on Encore at 11:30. Hopefully we'll watch it. Alright see ya' lata' *Mis$ing~L1nk*

Bob: My dear Mr. L1nk*: Well, I'll bet you can guess why I'm Marblehead, but in your case just what seems to be *Mis$ing? And L1nk* to what Patrick? L1nk* to what? Hmmmmm?????

Thanks for the tip on "Dr. Strangelove." As wacky as it is, it's closer to the truth than you should ever have to believe. One of the all time greatest movies. For many reasons beyond the message.

Hey! Enough of the chit-chat. Will you help me set up a home page or at least point me in the right direction? Actually, maybe you should tell me where your page is. Vo ist der *Mis$ing~L1nk*?

In a follow-up message, Bob wrote:

Patrick:

I have a friend who has a bunch of Soviet era memorabilia. When I learned you were studying the Cold War, I asked him if he had something you might find interesting. He gave me a Young Pioneer pin. The Young Pioneers were the Communist Party equivalent to the Scouts. I'll give the pin to your mom next time I see her. My friend says the YP's were affectionately known as the Order of the Red Brat, but I won't tell if you decide to wear it! Regards, – Marblehead

Bob still had an office in S.T. Olin Laboratory in the fall of 1996. He suggested that we have a picnic lunch on the roof of the building, so I brought some food one day and we made our way up to the top exit, passing through interesting infrastructure and HVAC systems. Emerging into the sun, we were treated to a glorious view of Cayuga Lake and the flaming colors of the peak leaf season.

The next day's exchange reflected our deepening feelings.

Subject: They dined in the most exotic places!
Bob: That was pretty cool. Maybe we should try it at night! Looking forward to your cooking and company. More later.

Jenny: It was more than pretty cool, it was absolutely glorious – the best view of the area I've ever gotten a chance at – glad we grabbed it together. And YES at night...a loaf of bread, a bottle of champagne, and thou beside me on the rooftop...I can almost taste it.

Rain on my roof right now...looks like we really timed it right.

Thanks for your steady communication, Bob. It's filling up an empty place in me. Talk to you soon.

Bob: I'm so glad you're having fun with these e-mails and that it's more than just fun. It means a great deal to me too. I really think we should skip the entertainment tomorrow and just talk. There is so much for us to share about who we are, how we hurt, what we want, what we need. If there are consequences to what we say or do we need to tell each other so we can talk about what that means. Call me this evening if you get a chance. I should be up until 10ish.

We did have many heart-to-hearts that fall. At that first dinner at his house, I told Bob that he treated me like a queen, and he answered that I should think of myself as a goddess; in return I dubbed him my archangel – yes, it was that bad, and as weeks went by, our relationship bloomed. Even astrological references weren't too much for us: Bob's a Taurus and I'm a Pisces.

Bob: Clear morning sky and your lucky stars shine down on you and yours. You are under the influence of Taurus high above. Expect pleasurable company.

Good day for productive meetings.

Food is particularly important to your interactions. You'll fall asleep with a smile on your face.

Jenny: I woke up this morning with a smile on my face, too. I thank my lucky stars. You are under the influence of the fishes deep in the sea, but I'll come out to meet you on the beach...You were right last night, I've already let myself in for it, so I might as well relax and enjoy the ride.

Are you proud of me? I figured out how to do a reply all by myself! Last night, when I said that I wanted to save some e-mail, Patrick showed me how to make a folder and put things in it. He suggested the name "Bob's Letters," and it's in the "top seceret (sic) documents" file he created on the desktop.

The Transformation of Sage

Bob and I planned a drive up Cayuga Lake to the Montezuma Wildlife Refuge early one morning, to see raptors and migrating birds, and Bob's old college stomping grounds in Oswego. We were also planning a holiday trip to Montreal, an easy five-hour drive from Ithaca, and a world-class city that neither of us had visited, that now is one of our favorites. We were falling hard but it felt easy.

Bob: Good mornin' again, Darlin'. I'm still feeling that warm glow in my chest. This is the most wonderful feeling. I can't say, "I've never felt this before," but I can say, "I've never felt it like this before." There is such a peaceful, satisfying, nourishing depth to the way I feel about you. I've waited a long, long time to get to this place and to think our journey is just begun.

Next week will be so much fun and our first serious journey together. Just a practice session for our trip to Montreal. Our first international trip to a place new to both of us. Our own private history. I'll repeat our toast from last night:

>I want to travel the world with you
>
>Enjoying the finest pleasures
>
>Sights, sounds, tastes and drink
>
>And at the end of all those journeys
>
>None will be finer
>
>Than the pleasure we give each other

I love you, my precious Goddess Jennifer – Blue Skies

The Transformation of Sage

I was a graduate student in French studies, but in Cornell's graduate system I was free to assemble a program for myself from different disciplines, and I incorporated ethnomusicology into my thesis project about Cajun Mardi Gras. I was taking a course in African traditional music, and one day I noticed some tribal customs on the cable news that I shared with Bob.

Subject: comfortable girths

Jenny: I learned something about human behavior while I was having a bowl of gumbo, regarding cultural norms of physical beauty: the eligible bachelors of the Dinka tribe in northern Africa are having their connubial festival, and in preparation have been "bulking up" for the last few months... to demonstrate that their herds of milk cows can support a new member of the household, they each consume around five gallons of milk a day, spiked with cow urine, which provides them with sufficient weight gain to attract a (presumably pleasantly plump) bride...

Bob: Once again, sure am glad I'm an American! And this isn't something I have to do to win your favor. Dear Goddess, will you settle for rack of lamb, pork tenderloin, chicken soup, pasta, sausage, etc? – Humble Servant

Jenny (*returning to a favorite theme*): A loaf of bread, a jug of wine and thou beside me in the wilderness – might make sense of the wilderness of life as we know it. Thanks for the sustenance, and for taking the path through the wilderness with me.

The Transformation of Sage

Bob: Peace & Happiness...throughout the land. That's the Creator's master plan. Well, I know it's throughout my heart anyway. Thinking of you. Talk to you soon. Good morning, Jennifer – Robert

On our weekend getaway, Bob picked up a lucky stone on the beach by Ontario Lake near Oswego, a little rounded glacial erratic of pink granite for me to keep as a touchstone when he was away on an upcoming business trip, our first separation.

Patrick usually took a bus to school, but the Monday morning after the drive to Montezuma and Oswego our systems failed, and I drove him to his well-loved Alternative Community School on West Hill. Now renamed after its longtime principal, Dr. Dave, as the Lehman Alternative School, the charter school's focus is on community service and inclusiveness, and it's a performing arts magnet. The only thing we didn't like about the school was driving through the notorious Octopus, an intersection that was improved recently when the city built two more bridges for the three roads that had formerly shared one on the west end of town. This morning, we were in for the drive across town, but that didn't diminish my effusive mood when I got back home:

Jenny: Good morning, Angel Robert. I woke at 7:30 to a dark, quiet house, and realized immediately that I was going to experience the Octopus in its full morning glory while taking the kid to school – looks like he turned off his alarm in his sleep, bless his heart.

The Transformation of Sage

What a weekend! I am glowing with peace and happiness myself. Life is truly good, and we deserve it. I'm looking forward to a productive week, warmed by the fire you lit at my altar.

Subject: Taking flight

Bob: Lots of things took flight this weekend. The birds at Montezuma National Wildlife Refuge and the hearts at Stundtner's Gorge for example. We didn't see any eagles or hawks in flight, but I feel like I'm soaring. So this is what they mean by "the incredible lightness of being."

Jenny: What a great movie! It fits in with the idea of spirits independent of corporeal entities, too, a critical concept. Still, I'm glad we visualize you as a rock to build on – I don't want to fly away yet, especially not now.

Bob: Well, started some laundry. Now I'm heading to the yard to toss the stick for Cilantro. Think I'll fire off one of my best cigars. Avo Uvesian. Tastes like café latte. It's a nice warm day to sit in the yard and savor the time we've spent together and think about seeing you play this evening and when we'll be together again and...

Life is good and I got it bad. I'm a lucky man. Soon come, my love – Robert P.

Before leaving on his business trip, Bob reassured me electronically...

Subject: Sweet Dreams

Most Beautiful Goddess Jennifer: Pleasant dreams and a sweet smile be yours all night long. Wake to my certain adoration shining through your window. Go forth with my shield of stone to protect you. Grant me an e-mail or two, I beseech thee. Think of dancing cheek to cheek. Your ever-loving acolyte, Robert

    I wrote a poem for Bob one morning, looking out over the snowy woods behind my little condo, invoking the Tibetan goddess of mercy who hears the cries of all humanity. He printed it out and wrote one day,

Good mornin', Darlin'. Seems like I have to write that if I can't whisper it in your ear. Listen hard enough and you'll hear me say it deep in your heart. I get up and read aloud your morning prayer every day now. I don't think you kept it, so...

> *...to the goddess of mercy:*
>
> *Peaceful wintry windowscape*
>
> *Every branch defined in white*
>
> *Imagining your strong arms around me*
>
> *Strength to believe*
>
> *Strength to persevere*
>
> *Strength to sustain our love*
>
> *Let it grow in tranquility*
>
> *Let it nourish ourselves and our loved ones*
>
> *Let it warm our souls through the long, cold nights*
>
> *And rise like the bright sun every day.*

My strong arms are around you always my beloved Goddess Jennifer
—Archangel Robert

The Transformation of Sage

Bob and I read our favorite poems to each other, shared our music, and told each other stories from the 40-some years we had been on the planet before we met. We began to believe in a future that held a place for our love, and Bob's messages reflect our growing sense of the rightness of the relationship. He sent me the classic John Donne love poem one morning, and we read it still sometimes, wondering at our good fortune.

The Good-Morrow

I wonder, by my troth, what thou and I

Did till we loved? Were we not weaned till then

But sucked on country pleasures, childishly

Or snorted we in the seven sleepers' den

'Twas so; but this, all pleasures fancies be

If ever any beauty I did see

Which I desired, and got, 'twas but a dream of thee.

And now good-morrow to our waking souls,

Which watch not one another out of fear;

For love all love of other sights controls

And makes one little room an everywhere

Let sea-discoverers to new worlds have gone

Let maps to other, worlds on worlds have shown

Let us possess one world; each hath one, and is one

The Transformation of Sage

My face in thine eye, thine in my appears

And true plain hearts do in the faces rest

Where can we find two better hemispheres

Without sharp north, without declining west

Whatever dies was not mixed equally;

If our two loves be one, or thou and I

Love so alike that none can slacken, none can die.

John Donne (1572-1631)

Isn't it amazing that John Donne wrote about my bedroom on Sunday mornings over 350 years ago? How'd he do that? I guess he loved a woman as much as I love you or near enough anyway.

Is there more?

> *More and more and more!*
>
> *Insatiable*
>
> *Incredible*
>
> *Undeniable*
>
> *Relentless*
>
> *Unquenchable*
>
> *Endless*
>
> *Immutable*
>
> *Boundless*
>
> *Unbelievable*

The Transformation of Sage

Transcendent

Predestined

Impulsive

Alluring

Exciting

Satisfying

Serendipitous

Joyous

Sensual

And more and more and more!

What a truly incredible weekend. A glorious anniversary. I can't believe I'm experiencing what I'm experiencing.

Now I know that the best days of my life are ahead of me. Thank you for revealing the lake to the mountain. Thank you for letting me share my memories both sweet and bitter. The Goddess Jennifer possesses healing powers. Praise be to the Goddess. I will worship her always.

With my deepest affection,
Ol' Blue Eyes

We found a rhythm in our short-distance love affair, traversing the back roads of the hill that separated our homes after dinner or at dawn. If we didn't see each other we talked on the phone; we laughed when, up on East Hill, I heard the train whistle downtown a few seconds after Bob did. We had lunch together

The Transformation of Sage

often, once on a lovely fall afternoon in the Cornell Plantations by the ponds.

And of course the work at Sage Hall went forward. Ezra Cornell is fondly referred to as "Uncle Ezra" in Ithaca, and in 1986 various student services joined forces to create the virtual interface that they call "Ask Uncle Ezra," to allow the Cornell community to ask questions about what they see and hear around campus. In October of 1996, one inquiring mind wanted to know...

Dear Uncle Ezra:

Why do I never see any work being done on Sage Hall, and when will it be finished?

[The question was forwarded to Bob, who responded: The drama of the Sage Hall project continues to unfold. You may not think so if you only walk by along Sage Avenue or Campus Road. But take a stroll along the Statler side of East Avenue and stop to look into the project site. You'll see five story walls seemingly floating in air, hovering over the people and machines busily working to create the foundations for the modern facility to be born within. You're not likely to ever see such a marvel of architecture and engineering again. Come and look.]

Bob's next project update was published in *FaCeS*, the award-winning newsletter for the Division of Facilities and Campus Services, and was edited by our friend Peggy Haine. Peggy is a local icon, the diva of a blues band in the 1980's and a favorite auctioneer and MC at fundraising events. I've known her since my early band days, as a fellow chick bass player. When Bob

The Transformation of Sage

and I celebrated our wedding in 1998, Peg and her husband Peter Hoover, also a musician (and a cider-maker too), made sumptuous hop wreathes for us to wear!

Bob was excited about working with her on the story, and it was the first update that I had seen, since having been added to the distribution list.

From: Peggy Haine

Dear Bob,

I've edited your very good story for FaCeS. Please take a look and make sure I haven't massacred it or left out anything important. Correct any mistakes and send it back to me by tomorrow afternoon, if possible. Many thanks. What a good writer you are! Thanks for contributing to FaCeS.

Cheers!

Peg

[*Cheers to you, Peg!*

Wow! I'm collaborating with Peggy Haine! Way cool!

I'm flattered you like what I'm writing. I changed one sentence slightly and added another because I was writing late at night and left one group out. Please, please tell me it fits.

My pleasure – Regards, Bob]

The Transformation of Sage

Update 10
10/14/96

After nearly six years of residency on the Baker/Olin project, I've moved my office from Baker Laboratory to Beacon's project trailer on the Sage Hall site. It's great to be in the thick of it, but I have to admit to a touch of sadness at leaving my palatial digs in the Department of Chemistry.

They weren't always palatial. Sharon Wargo and I started out in an office so small that we had to take turns backing our chairs away from our desks. Lucky for us, the floor-by-floor renovations in S. T. Olin finally got down to the first floor (precisely on schedule, of course) and we were "forced" to relocate to a freshly renovated office on the 2nd floor. After three years of having to stand up to see anything more than the sky out the slot that was our window, we shared a 19-foot long vista of treetops and North Campus. Beebe Lake was in view, and once a falcon flew by at eye level.

But all good things come to pass and we spent a yearlong stint in a windowless office before moving to a huge suite of offices in 150 Baker Lab. Sharon is extremely busy closing out the project and will probably move to our Sage office after the first of the year.

The folks at Beacon are adjusting to my presence very nicely. It really helps to be able to walk a few steps and deal with something pressing, be it trivial or budget stretching. The only problem is the candy dish won't hold more than a small handful of Atomic Fireballs!

The Transformation of Sage

Sage Hall is looking particularly dramatic these days. Selective removals of the old building are complete and all that remains is to remove the huge piles of bricks, lumber, and pipe. The starkness of the remaining structure is head turning. It's fun to see so many passersby rubberneck, stop to point and gesture, or snap a photo.

And what of the lost second verse of that old chestnut "A Modern Project Manager?" The first extolled the virtues of the support I get from my colleagues in Facilities & Campus Services. The second sings the praises of the rest of the University.

It's hard to be the "very model of a modern project manager" if you don't have a project to manage. Wow! Has the Johnson Graduate School of Management got a project or what?

Thanks to the vision of former Dean Alan Merton, the faculty and the JGSM Advisory Council and the generosity of many, many donors, Sage Hall will become the most interesting and challenging building transformation ever undertaken on our campus. The historic landmark will have its worn exterior restored and give up its shabby interior to become one of the premier business school facilities in the world.

I'm still not up to speed on all the players at JGSM, but that's only because John McKeown makes it unnecessary for me to deal with a cast of thousands (well, tens anyway). John has been our very capable client interface to the project since its inception. He, Eric Dicke, and I serve as the executive project management team in a novel arrangement suggested by Hal Craft. John's integrity has led

The Transformation of Sage

to the Johnson School's unprecedented access to project management decision making.

The faculty is strongly represented through the Building Committee and Bob Libby as Chair. Bob can be quite blunt when reminding me of the School's priorities, and that is very refreshing to a project manager who can be equally blunt.

My most fun interactions with the Johnson School come from Steve Sharratt, Donna Spinella, and Catherine Davidson. They provide a level of professionalism to fund raising, alumni affairs, and communications that is completely consistent with the well-deserved reputation of the Johnson School. Through them I get to reach out around the world and apparently have acquired a few fans. Next week, I'll get to meet the Advisory Council and give them a tour of the project.

Speaking of professionalism, one of my greatest pleasures since coming to Cornell 16 years ago has been my all too infrequent collaborations with Shirley Egan, Associate University Counsel. Shirley led the effort to defend us against the attempt by the Heritage Coalition to halt the Sage project. With the intellectual gusto and cool-headed thoughtfulness (good humor, too) she brings to the bar, one wonders why anyone would bother to challenge us legally once Shirley is assigned the case.

The Sage project has attracted quite a bit of notice in the press. When I need advice about that inevitable contact, David Stewart and John Gutenberger in Community Relations help me to present the facts in a clear and concise way. David has also provided

The Transformation of Sage

flattering encouragement to these missives. Gutie's savvy insights into the local scene are almost as welcome as his humor. He's rescued more than one stressful day with his e-mail.

The demanding schedule of the project has caused us to work early and stay late quite often and that includes several weekends. The Sage site is not only prominent. It's across the street from a hotel. The managing director, James Hisle, has been very understanding of the need to be noisy early in the morning and late into the evening. The maintenance director, Horst Albrecht, provides us with generous access to the Hotel's roofs to shoot progress photos [*by Jon Reis*]. They lend practical credence to the Statler School's leadership of the hospitality industry.

As I said, it takes a very significant part of the Cornell Community to make a "modern project manager." I'm also investigating a rumored third verse about people outside the University. If I keep this up, you'll all be singing Gilbert & Sullivan!

Next week Poangeli Construction will start the excavation of the basement. In a couple of weeks, we'll be starting to rebuild Sage Hall and a whole new drama will unfold.

[Shirley K. Egan: Hi Bob - How funny, thoughtful, and kind you are! Thank you again for being you. When I open up my mail and there are the usual 4 dozen messages awaiting me, if I see one from you, I open it first because I know I'll laugh and start the day on the right side of the street. And I especially enjoyed the reference to the wonderful song from Pirates of Penzance. My 15-year old played the Pirate King in it last summer in Canada, so the lyrics are all fresh in my mind! I

The Transformation of Sage

really laughed because for their last performance they substituted freely as appropriate in the song also!

Before he was finished he called it the "Privates of Pennance"!

Thanks again for keeping me on your mailing list for Sage updates. Take care. Shirley]

Around this time Bob spent an evening with his friend Keith, who was going through a marital separation (happily, Keith and Cathy found each other a few years later, another love story of the Finger Lakes). Bob took along a CD of the Highwoods to play for Keith, and wrote to me the next morning:

Finished up the weekend a bit late last night with Keith. Late for Monday morning and the amount of bourbon we commiserated over anyway. Tears, fears, regrets and finally hope for feeling better about our relationships. I know I sure do.

Keith enjoyed listening to the CD, but he was ready for some R n' R at the same song as you were Saturday night. I love listening to it knowing that gal pickin' & singin' is you so long ago. I can hear the youth in your voice. Keith invites you to play bass at his place Friday. I think I told you a bunch of his friends and he get together and rock out. Actually, they rock in and not "out" in public. Probably a good thing, too. It's joyous though!

Well, late for work. See you soon. Talk to you sooner. Thinking about you a lot.

The Transformation of Sage

Not many mornings went by without a phone call between Bob and me at this point, usually followed up with e-mails during the day and dinner together at night, at my house during the week and at Bob's on the weekend when Patrick had a sleep-over. Since Patrick and I shared a computer, I had seen Bob's messages to him.

Jenny: Good morning and thanks for all the messages and shared feelings. I made a mistake and read the message you sent to Patrick – I'll have to apologize, but it sure was sweet to witness you reaching out to him like that.

Bob: I'll try to make the header reference obviously addressed to him so you can develop the shared mailbox, but maintain privacy. If he sees me sending mail to him that you don't open, maybe he will respect your unopened mail. I'll still be a little circumspect in what I write.

Jenny: I realized, though, when I said goodnight, that he still has some apprehensions about a new relationship developing for me...he told me he loved me more than anything in the world. I reassured him that he is my top priority. I know that he really needs me here, in more than a perfunctory way.

Bob: Thank you for sharing his apprehensions. I certainly understand and support that he is your first priority. I hear what he means to you. Lucky you. Lucky him. I hope we can all figure out how to keep the relationships healthy and reinforcing of the mother/child union. Nothing more important in the world.

Jenny: "The problem revolves around achieving a quiet heart." So says the I Ching. It's a problem I've been circling around for a long time, and attempting to confront face-to-face with a sense of some urgency this year. Yet I feel it's not just the bad times that revolve around this problem, the good times need that inner tranquility too, to fulfill their potential. You have lit a fire in me, and I will be tending it; but I'm visualizing it as a place I can go without seeing you or touching you, or even writing to you, where I can warm myself with a sense of caring. It's not separate from the physical passion, it's a deepening aspect of that and other shared experience, and a place where I can take care of myself and my own.

Bob: Yes. I share your sense of some urgency in addressing the problem this year. I'm feeling the warmth of the fire without feeling like I'm going to be consumed. There's an album I really enjoy called "The Restful Mind." I'm thinking we're creating a new title called the "Restful Heart." What a grand collaboration, Jennifer.

Jenny: All the same...you could be thinking about a night you might like to come here for dinner. No dance floor, but we could watch a video and snuggle on the couch.

Bob: "Ready when you are CB." Good week for me. Use your judgment as to whether or not it's too much face time for Patrick.

Jenny: A flock of geese just flew by, heading south. Good weather for curling up with one's books. Hope your day goes smoothly.

Bob: Got to get to work here. Let's see, mostly light week, then facility survey Saturday at 10am. Move piano that afternoon. Fireside concert later in the evening. And then more composing. Heart don't fail me now!

Keith had been looking for a home for his estranged wife's piano, and Bob took it in for me to play. The facility survey scheduled for Saturday was of the State Theater, a vaudeville

The Transformation of Sage

venue in downtown Ithaca built in 1928 that was threatened with demolition. The State had been converted into a movie theater, but finally couldn't compete with the megatheaters at the mall, and it's owner, Joe Ciaschi, threatened to take it down and build a parking lot on the main street site. It was the last standing theater out of seventeen that once operated in the city, but was desperately in need of a new roof and other renovations to bring it up to code, an amount of work that couldn't be paid for with revenue from performances alone. A group of people from the Finger Lakes Grassroots Festival, including me, attempted to convince the community that it was worth saving the theater and operating it as a performing arts center. The effort was ultimately successful when Historic Ithaca, a non-profit organization whose mission is to preserve designated historic buildings in Ithaca, bought the structure in 1998.

The State Theater preservation had been a topic of conversation at Micawber's, where advocates of the cause met to discuss strategies. Bob decided to join the effort, and invited an elite group of his facilities colleagues from Cornell, all music lovers and community-minded men, to meet at the theater and investigate the scope of the renovation project in late October. Bob forwarded me the invitation he had sent to his friends:

10/21/1996
Bob : Here's the invite! Looks like most can make it.

The Transformation of Sage

To: Art Stern, Jeff Lallas, Bruce Frantz, Paul Sarokwash, Martin Kelly, Randy Lacey, Jim Bucko, Jim Gibbs:

Subject: State Theater - Facility Survey

Dear Volunteer Facilities Professionals for the Preservation and Development of Historic State Theater in Ithaca (VFP2DHSTI or fiptodisty for short):

Thanks for volunteering to crawl around the State Theater. To recap – this effort is in support of a new management group (based all or in part on the Grassroots Festival Board) that is attempting to negotiate an agreement with Joe Ciaschi for a new mortgage.

The new management group will need to have a good idea of what condition the building is in so they can develop a capital plan for maintenance and improvements. That's the task ahead of us.

I'd like to try to pull this off this Saturday (10/26) starting at 10am. I'd guess that two hours would do the trick. Then I'll take our list of projects, put some flesh on the bones, and circulate a draft. Who's up for what should prove to be a very interesting facility audit? Soooo...when people ask us, "Where are you guys from?" we reply, "We're from Fiptodisty and as we all know, that covers a lot of territory." To which most people go, "Huh?"

As Bernie Milton [a local favorite performer and soul singer] says, "Bye, Baby."

Coitio ergo sum – Robertus (sage advisor, late 20th Century)

[Jenny: You are the greatest! Thank you in advance to all of your music-loving friends, too. What can I say? Free tickets all around, obviously, but...is there more? I bet there will be. And a return visit to

The Transformation of Sage

Key West would be excellent this weekend. Can't wait to dance with you again on our first dance floor.

Patrick and I viewed the tape he made of Dr. Strangelove. It is more impressive than I remember it, and I helped interpret the more obscure references for him; I guess his teacher agreed to let the class watch it one week. What a great school!

I better stop before I get too effusive...Buenas noches, hasta mañana mi amor.]

Bob: Go ahead! Get too effusive. I love it because I know it's genuine and that I've done/said something to please you.

Don't you love it when a plan comes together? I think I can speak for my friends when I say we're really excited to be part of your team. It's important for our community that this effort be successful. With your gentle hand on the helm, we'll sail on!

I brought bagels and coffee for the crew that Saturday morning, and enjoyed watching the men think through the massive project. I didn't climb the ladder to the roof, but otherwise followed the group through the dilapidated structure. The documents produced by the facility survey that they undertook were vital to the various entities that would eventually ameliorate the "State of the State." I wrote them a thank you note the next week:

From: Jenny
To: Fiptodisties

The Transformation of Sage

Thank you all so much for giving up a chunk of your weekend to survey the state of the State. It was impressive to watch such an expert group put its collective mind together to evaluate the facility. Any energy you may have individually or collectively for this project is welcome, and be sure to contact me personally for those back-stage passes when the time comes...Who would you like to see play there? We welcome input on that as well.

Sincerely, Jenny Cleland

It took many years for the building's condition to be stabilized, but I'm happy to report that the State Theatre of Ithaca New York has been in operation since 2001; and while I didn't end up becoming further involved with the theater, Art Stern (of the Fiptodisties) is a long-standing member of the State's Board of Directors.

Requests for information on Sage Hall came in to Bob, as he struggled with the challenges of the project:

11/14/96
From: Deborah Chilson [*Eric Dicke's Administrative Assistant*]

Bob:

In Eric's absence could you please write a paragraph for the Sage web page and e-mail it to Wendy Fuller? You're so good at this! Thanks.

[*Ooooops! I forgot to do this for you Wendy. Forty lashes with a wet noodle. I would ask that I be allowed to peel it off the back of my head when you're done though. Bob*]

View from the roof of the Statler Hotel, October 29, 1996
© Jon Reis Photography

The Transformation of Sage

Update 11
11/21/96

The drama of the Sage Hall project continues to unfold. You may not think so if you only walk by along Sage Avenue or Campus Road. But take a stroll along the Statler side of East Avenue and stop to look into the project site. You'll see five story walls seemingly floating in air, hovering over the people and machines busily working to create the foundations for the modern facility to be born within. You're not likely to ever see such a marvel of architecture and engineering again. Come and look.

For those of you who can't swing by the site, here's what's going on.

Paoangeli Construction (Pogo) has several pieces of excavating equipment digging and grading to the new basement elevations. In some places, we're down almost 20 feet below the old basement floor elevations. A nearly constant parade of dump trucks is entering and leaving the site. The material being removed is a fine, brown silt for the most part, but there is also a lower layer of blue clay. When it rains, both are very gooey which is why there are long trails of mud leaving the site. It's a constant battle to contain or filter muddy storm water runoff.

In a classic example of unforeseen conditions, the bedrock is lower than expected at one end of the site and higher than expected at the other. This means deeper digging or drilling to bedrock for footings or caissons at the low end and much harder excavation at the high end. As a fossil hound, I wish I had the luxury to stop the work and explore the exposed bedrock. Some layers are rich with the remains of the animals and plants from the ancient ocean [*400 million years*

The Transformation of Sage

ago in the Devonian Age]. What will remain of Sage that many years in the future?

The contractor, Welliver-McGuire, is building and pouring footers and piers to support the new structural steel. The workers really earn their pay on a job like this. It's a feverish pace and at times a dangerous ballet to maintain your awareness of what's around you, and hear over the din of vehicles, hammers and power tools to avoid being run over. Smooth soled boots are slippery. Lug soled boots accumulate twice their size and four times their weight in mud. This time of year it's damp or cold and often both. Sleep and a regular paycheck aren't the only salves for the exhaustion, but they're the most rewarding.

T. G. Miller is the surveyor on the project. Targets have been placed all over the exterior of the old walls to monitor stability. So far, no movement has been detected. Building a new structure within an existing one has proved to be every bit as difficult as we thought. The inner structural grid can be laid out and dimensioned, but what is the distance to the exterior wall and mansard roof? We've only had access to measure the hundreds of critical points since the demolition was completed. The thickness and plumbness of walls varies considerably. The mansard roofs are not all uniformly angled or dimensioned either. Every measurement is important if the new steel is to fit.

The days are flying by and it's hard to believe that Friday can arrive so quickly. We're grateful and wishing for another day to get things done at the same time. May 1, 1998 is just around the corner. Got to go. Talk to you soon.

Bob

The Transformation of Sage

Bob struggled to keep his tone positive, as difficulties, not the least of them the exceptionally bad weather that winter, continued to mount. But the challenges inherent in renovating an old building, and particularly the melon-balling of Sage Hall, were met with persistence and perseverance, and as always Bob's deep, soothing tone comes through in his report to the community.

Update 12
12/12/96

I know it's not news, but it's Ithacating again! Cool, wet and gray. Can't remember when we last had a day of sunshine. Beacon's Superintendent, Claude LeBlanc keeps a daily log, but it would take too long to read back through it to find that brief shining moment.

Our project trailer must be one of the dirtiest offices on earth. Consumer Reports advises against purchasing maintenance agreements and extended warrantees, but we're getting our money's worth on our copier agreement. We may have to make room for the technician to sleep here!

The weather is slowly chipping away at contractor enthusiasm and our schedule. It's not insurmountable and we still anticipate finishing on schedule, but we'd really appreciate a string of warm, sunny days to make up a bit of what we've lost.

Mass excavation is nearly complete. The skill of the equipment operators on this project is awesome. One minute two machines are collaborating to push a ten ton boulder out of the hole and the next they're precisely shaving the surface to dead level within an inch of final grade. It's amazing to watch them excavate and build at the

The Transformation of Sage

same time so that they can crawl out of the thirty-foot deep hole. Every time I stop to watch them briefly, I see them make some maneuver that knocks my socks off. Best show for sidewalk superintendents in town!

The project team is working very hard to meet the structural challenges presented by building a new structure inside an existing one. Picture in your mind the exterior walls and mansard roofs of old Sage Hall. They wrap around 3 and a half sides of what will be the new building footprint. Inside, there is a deep hole to form the new basement floor that is deeper than the foundations of the original building.

The design team precisely laid out the grid of the new structural steel, but it wasn't possible to know with any precision where the old walls and mansards were in relation to the new steel. The old walls are derived from multiple additions to the original Sage. None of the walls are square or plumb. The angle of the mansards varies considerably.

The new structural grid must be connected to the old structures so a great deal of time is being expended to measure where everything is. This information must be passed on to the steel detailers who draw up the pieces to be fabricated. The lengths and/or angles of hundreds of pieces of steel are being custom measured so they will fit.

Tight floor to ceiling heights add to the challenge. Modern heating, ventilation, air conditioning, electrical, plumbing, sprinklers, and telecommunications services must be crammed within the constraints of the existing structure. Hundreds of penetrations of the structural steel must be laid out with great precision so that everything will fit.

The Transformation of Sage

We're going to find out how precisely we're able to plan and build in three dimensions, that's for sure!

The winter solstice is upon us. Only a few more days of decreasing daylight and then we turn the corner. I'm taking two weeks off starting the 21st so I'll get to experience the change from my home. In my yard, I always hear the chickadees excitedly announcing the longer days just after the New Year. Next year, I'll imagine them singing, "the steel is here-here-here."

Wishing you a peaceful holiday season,

Bob

Patrick spent the holidays with my parents in western Pennsylvania. They were second parents to him, and he enjoyed seeing his old friends from our former hometown. Bob and I took advantage of the child-free time to drive up to Montreal, a scenic five-hour drive from Ithaca, whose Old World charm is greatly appealing to this Europhile. We stayed at the Marriott Château Champlain, nicknamed the Caterpillar for its design that provides every room a bay window. It's a good choice in winter, because you can take an elevator from the hotel lobby to the underground city that keeps life going in a brutal climate. One night, with a glistening view of the city lights below us, we took the boldest move and promised to marry each other. Many visits to Quebec later, we feel we've never made a better decision.

While our relationship grew, the drama continued at Sage Hall; the steel contractor fell further and further behind schedule,

The Transformation of Sage

threatening the completion date of the entire project. Of course the weather didn't help, but there were procedural problems as well, as Bob laid out in the following eyes-only report.

1/9/97
Subject: Sage Hall – Confidential

To: Eric Dicke, John McKeown, Ruben Rogers, Steve Wright, Hal Craft

Gentlemen:

This heads up may tend to knot your stomach a bit. DON'T PANIC!

At Tuesday's job meeting Beacon's construction manager stated the following: the current schedule for steel erection indicates completion in mid-April versus the original schedule of mid-March. Thus the project is 4-5 weeks behind schedule. However, Beacon still sees adequate time remaining in the project to accomplish the work in time for the May 1, 1998 JGSM occupancy date. Overall the project is on schedule, but that is less assured than it once was.

The immediate problem seems to rest squarely with the structural steel (engineer – Silman; subcontractor – Rome Iron Group, contract value $2,577,000). Rome is currently starting with their third detailer. All three detailers have claimed that the drawings are incomplete and they aren't in the business of filling in the blanks or burning up time and money asking for information and waiting for it.

Rome has started making claims against Beacon for time and money. Unfortunately for Rome, Beacon says they have not followed the terms of their subcontract for notification, etc. removing the possibility of Beacon correcting. Beacon will do everything in their power to help, but basically it's Rome's problem financially.

The Transformation of Sage

Beacon is making much the same argument to Cornell for compensation. Ruben, Eric and I met with their Project Executive Bob Eckstein and Project Manager John Hermans Tuesday morning to listen to their interpretation of the story. In their opinion the drawings are not up to the standards of the industry and they are starting to provide supporting documentation. I've just read through some correspondence between Rome and various detailers (one who quit before he started). The unanimous opinion is that the drawings are incomplete.

One of Hillier's architects stated last month that if we thought the structure was hard, wait 'til we got to the interior. Summarizing what he said: The only interior part of the building that is fully detailed and dimensioned is the atrium. Once The Hillier Group [*THG*] was through the structural crunch they would start a series of sketches that would head off the requests for information [*RFI's*] that were inevitable from the interior subs. That sounds like the "incomplete drawing" problem is not confined to the structural engineer.

To compound things, Hillier is also struggling to maintain a reasonable turn-around time for RFI's and submittal review. Basically, one bright, but inexperienced construction administrator is the very small needle the whale must pass through. Things have improved, but we'll have a serious log jam once we get a little further along if THG doesn't figure out how to parallel process the flow of work.

These issues (not always substantiated) have been communicated to THG for several months now. Hillier's project manager, Peter Hoggan, will meet with Ruben, Eric and me Friday 1/17 to discuss the current situation, the allegations, and a path forward. The whole project

The Transformation of Sage

team (Beacon, THG, JGSM, CU) will convene 2/11 for a regularly scheduled quarterly review.

Critical issues for us:

- Steel Erection – THG must keep the RFI/submittal process flowing smoothly. Beacon is going to great lengths to fill in the gaps by hiring a local structural engineer. Rome doesn't have the financial strength to gamble on extra expenses to accelerate if they may not get reimbursed. Beacon will keep on top of this. The weather must be kind.

- Schedule – The May 1st date is very important to JGSM. Before the recent *US News and World Report* ranking [*JGSM was rated in the top 20 graduate business schools in 1997*], it wasn't. Now, they feel they must have a completed world-class facility to hold graduation festivities so that [the new building] is the last impression the next class to be surveyed would have of Cornell. It's doable, but assumes we can get the steel up reasonably close to mid-April.

- Financial – Thus far, there are probably $250K of real costs that must be assumed by somebody. Not a killer to the major players including us, but in my opinion it's Beacon's and/or Hillier's responsibility.

- Team – This may be the most difficult to keep from melting down. Some staff at Beacon and THG are really stretched to the limits. The potential for finger pointing is mind-boggling. So far, there has been a fair amount of integrity on everyone's part, but the tension is building. I will pay very close attention to this and take appropriate steps to intervene as necessary. There's nothing like adversity, as they say.

The Transformation of Sage

Next steps:

I'll be meeting with Eric Monday, Ruben and Steve next Thursday to discuss and plan strategy. I will send Peter Hoggan the supporting documentation Beacon is providing on the accusations of incomplete drawings so he can understand why we're concerned. By next Thursday, I will have our project budget snapshot and projection tools completed so we can see where we're going and try alternative scenarios. Beacon and I are discussing Rome's status on a daily basis. I will keep you posted.

Bob

    Bob and his team took advantage of the university's winter break to erect a crane into the project on January 11. East Avenue was closed, and as the monstrous machine moved down the road towards Sage Hall, a crowd gathered to watch the spectacle. We got a lot more excitement than anticipated, when Claude Leblanc, stationed in the pit to take photos of the installation, had to jump out of the way as the crane operator lost control! Bob described the moment of panic in his subsequent update:

Update 13
1/21/97

This just in: Birders in the Cornell Community report an astounding change in the behavior of the common black-capped chickadees that are frequent visitors to bird feeders across the region. For the past week, instead of their usual song, "chick-a-dee-dee-dee," they have been heard singing, "the-steel-is-here-here-here!" This highly

The Transformation of Sage

unusual sound seems to be loudest in the vicinity of the East Avenue and Campus Road intersection on the Cornell Campus.

The Rome Iron group sent the first loads of the new structural steel to the site on Monday January 13th. The steel erector, Brownell Management Corp., has worked daily to erect steel on the western end of the building. Weather has ranged from freezing rain to sub-zero temperatures, but the steel workers have toughed it out to keep the work flowing.

I personally paid tribute to them for hanging in there in the bitter cold when most of the other contractors had to call it quits. The towering walls of the old Sage provide shelter from the westerly winds, but steel this cold could easily rip the flesh from bare skin. Hmmmm, maybe that's why beards are so popular with steel workers. We're talking "icicles hanging from the whiskers" cold. Not a job for me as I can't seem to work without sticking my tongue out the corner of my mouth. One false move and I'd be stuck there until Spring!

Before the steel arrived, we had to get something into the hole to lift it off the trucks and hoist it up. On Saturday the 11th, a 100 ton crane was partially assembled in front of Uris Hall and moved down East Avenue to a specially constructed ramp into the basement of Sage. Traffic was halted for about an hour as the crane slowly made its way. It doesn't look quite so big down in the hole, but this thing is almost as wide as the street. Final assembly of the boom took place in the hole and stretched from the western end out onto half of East Avenue.

Once turned and poised at the top of the ramp, we all carefully checked and checked again to make sure it was lined up properly before BACKING down the ramp. That's right. The operator had to

The Transformation of Sage

back this huge contraption down a steep ramp, barely wider than the crane. About half way down his foot slipped and the crane rolled freely and quickly. Beacon superintendent Claude LeBlanc can move surprisingly fast when chased by a big crane. Did he hold the camera steady for the dramatic photo?

Paolangeli Construction has completed the mass excavation. Almost 2,000 cubic yards of earth and rock were removed from the interior of Sage. Pogo used over 600 cubic yards of gravel fill to create the ramp. That material will be used to backfill in the basement.

By the end of the week all of the footers, piers and caissons will be complete and ready to receive the structural steel. Welliver-McGuire is pouring new basement walls and they should also be complete by week's end.

The Beacon project trailer is turning out to be just cozy enough on the coldest days. My feet don't seem to stay warm, but maybe when my project coordinator, Sharon Wargo, moves in, our high powered conversations will make the difference. Sharon is busy closing out our previous project at Baker Lab/S. T. Olin Chemistry Research. That's the project where the City of Ithaca's former mayor, Ben Nichols, held up our building permit to "persuade" the University to contribute higher payments in lieu of taxes. He was really aiming at Sage so it's another thought to warm the trailer. Sharon and I are still working and he's not!

Write to you soon,

Bob

[From: John C. Gutenberger: Bob: Thanks for these great updates – I hope you are compiling them into a book. I semi-collect signed first *edition books and your tome would make a great and unique addition. I now look forward to your reports as much as the arrival of my subscription to* Beaver Monthly *[now* Canada's History*]. Gutie*]

[Gutie, you're a wild man. You have my promise of the signed first edition, but the question is, "Will I have to retire first? Who owns the book? CU or me?"]

[*Bob:*

1. no

2. don't tell 'em]

    Bob's next report recounts the painfully slow progress of the project, which suffered delays resulting from the poor performance of Beacon's steel subcontractor, Rome Iron Group. Obstacles to the other contractors' adherence to their own time schedules cascaded as they were forced to work around the delayed steel delivery. Bob's audience was ready for an update, but he was concerned about public perceptions that could hinder support for the project. Responding to this request for the next episode in the Sage saga, Bob acknowledged that he needed to try, at least, to put a positive spin on the story.

2/13/97
From: Jackie Fenton [*now Beal*]

Hi Bob, the FaCeS committee is wondering if you, in your ever-eloquent writing style, would be interested in giving us another update for the next publication now in the works.

The Transformation of Sage

The last update I seem to have kept is from January. Have you done a February update (that I must have trashed – whoops), and if not, will you be doing one soon? The next issue is coming out in March and we discussed a February 19 (or so) deadline.

Let me know what you think. Thanks!

Jackie Fenton
Project Coordinator, PDC Shops

[Jackie: Ugh! Relax. You didn't trash anything. I've been dragging my feet about this because I can't seem to put a bright, shiny spin on the steel situation. In spite of your kind words about my writing style, I'm struggling to find a way to tell the story without creating a bunch of fallout. I'll give it a whirl. Just another interesting challenge! Bob]

Update 14
2/23/97

Bob, what's with those Sage project news e-mails? Haven't seen one for a loooooong time.

Well, I've written sevearl, but mi sphell check has bin brokrin and I was gist too embearesd to send them out with mistooks in them.

Sure, Bob.

Would you believe that sometimes a project can get so stressed that it's painful to write cheerful reports for general consumption? Here's the inside scoop:

When last I wrote (January 21st), the structural steel had just arrived. The subcontractor, Rome Iron Group, was two months late according to the original schedule, but Beacon felt that overall this netted out to about four weeks and could be easily made up to meet the occupancy date of May 1, 1998.

The rest of the winter Rome continued to do (or not do) things that put themselves further and further behind schedule. They delivered the steel in irregular spurts, reducing the efficiency of their very capable erector (Brownell) and frustrating the heck out of the project team. Every time we thought we had a handle on the situation, Rome would slip us up.

Since then, Rome has gotten all the steel here and it is substantially complete, but they are three months behind their original scheduled completion date of March 15th. Needless to say this has caused Beacon to scramble quite a bit to recover the lost time. You can imagine how stressful it's been for all of us to see a mild winter wasted by delayed steel deliveries.

So how are we getting back on schedule? Beacon has developed a strategy of resequencing the work that might best be described as parallel processing. Instead of waiting for all the steel to be done and working on one floor at a time, we've been working on all the floors simultaneously. Steel erection took place in quadrants from west to east. As soon as the steel work was complete in the first quadrant and had progressed enough in the second for other trades to work safely in the first, we started rough mechanical and electrical installations and poured concrete slabs.

The net result of the resequencing is that Beacon has recovered two months of the schedule. That gets us back to one month behind schedule, but there's less time to make it up. Now what?

View from the roof of the Statler Hotel, January 29, 1997
© *Jon Reis Photography*

The Transformation of Sage

Beacon's project engineer, Jon Pinto [*who had worked for Beacon before he graduated in 1996 from Cornell's Engineering Cooperative Program, only to stay at Cornell for the duration of the Sage project*] has teased out key tasks all along the critical path of the project schedule and by prudently reducing the number of days for each task, Beacon can bring the end date back to the original schedule. Now we need to get subcontractor buy-in so we have more than a paper success. Next week we'll meet with the subs and begin turning the promise of getting back on track into a reality.

For the first time in the last five months, we're all beginning to breath easier. We're not out of the woods by a long shot, but we're starting to feel like that light at the end of the tunnel is an "on-time celebration" and not an oncoming freight train!

There's much more I want to tell you about what's going on with Sage, but I'll save that for my next project news. As they say in Jamaica, "Soon come!"

Bob

[*From: John C. Gutenberger: Hey, every train needs a good engineer, conductor, steward, and coal shoveler, glad you are aboard to fill all those shoes. Now just remember to pull slowly and gently into the station so the passengers don't even realize they have come to a stop. Gutie*]

[Have you ever tried to slowly stop a $38.2 Million dollar train? Me neither. I'm hoping I can stop it on this side of zero, but there may be a case of whiplash or two. Probably my backside! Marblehead]

Photograph of Sage College Front Entrance

*Courtesy of the Division of Rare and Manuscript Collections,
Cornell University Library*

Chapter 6: To the Coming Man and Woman

Soon a new challenge was on the horizon, as the project team prepared to remove the historic time capsule that had been placed in the original cornerstone at the dedication ceremony of Sage Hall in 1873. Second-year Johnson School MBA student Tatiana Rosak had come across a mention of the cornerstone in *The History of Women at Cornell*, a handbook put together by the Cornell Women's Resource Center, which referred to a letter that Ezra Cornell had placed inside the cornerstone during the building's dedication in 1873. The contents of that letter remained a mystery, since Ezra Cornell had made no copy of it. "I knew the building was being renovated, so I asked the Cornell administration whether we could open up the cornerstone and take a peek at this letter," said Rosak in the *Chronicle*, when she attended the cornerstone rededication in October of 1997.

In spite of the extensive masonry restoration and renovation of Sage, the project had no need to disturb the cornerstone. However, the Johnson School decided to act on Ms. Rosak's suggestion, and in late February a plan to open the cornerstone began to take shape, as documented in John McKeown's and Bob's e-mails.

To the Coming Man and Woman

Bob:

Pete Capalongo [*foreman of the CU Mason Shop*] will be contacting you to take a look at getting the historic material from behind the cornerstone. We will pay for this effort out of our normal operating funds. We are almost certainly going to want to proceed. I will let you know shortly.

John

[John: Pete and I looked at this and have the following recommendation.

The cornerstone is too massive to pull directly from the front. Pete proposes to set up scaffold in the entranceway and remove brick from behind the stone. A few bricks could reveal if what we're looking for is behind or under the cornerstone. We suspect that it is a hollowed out stone, and that could be a real problem for removal. Be prepared to spend as much as $2,000 to carefully explore and restore. Actually, I'd button it up and let Beacon do the final repointing in accordance with the rest of the brick restoration.

What do we know about the placement of the documents, etc? As much details, photos, etc. would be very helpful to Pete. Bob]

Unfortunately all the information they had was the list of contents that Charles Babcock had read at the dedication ceremony in 1873:

1. Parchments bearing the date of the laying of the stone, and the names of the architect and builder.

2. Copies of the *Register*.

To the Coming Man and Woman

3. Laws and documents relating to the University.

4. The *Albany Evening Journal Almanac* of 1873.

5. The *New York Daily Times.*

6. The Ithaca daily papers.

7. *The Era.* [Cornell's student paper]

8. A letter addressed by Mr. Cornell "To the Coming Man and Woman."

Nevertheless, the team decided to attempt to retrieve the documents from the stone, and began to work through the process of what seemed just another unforeseen condition at the time, but turned out to be one of the most unique aspects of the renovation.

Bob:

I will be putting in a request through Customer Service for Pete Capalongo to remove the contents of the cornerstone. The University Archivist [*Elaine Engst*] and I would like to be there for the removal.

John

[John: Pete is setting up scaffold this afternoon and tomorrow will start to remove bricks from the backside of the wall where the cornerstone is located. Don't have any way of knowing how long before they hit pay dirt or decide it's a dry hole. We'll keep you posted. Bob]

The removal was set to go forward quickly to keep the project on time. Bob copied the University Archivist on his

To the Coming Man and Woman

message to the team about opening the cornerstone, so that she could plan to attend.

3/5/97

We think we've found the secret hideaway. It's inside the cornerstone. Pete Capalongo will have things set so that we can all witness the final unveiling at 1pm on Tuesday. See you there!

[*Elaine Engst: How exciting! Do you mean Tuesday, March 11 or tomorrow (Thursday), March 6. Has anyone called the News Bureau to tell them? It's certainly newsworthy.*]

Sorry I wasn't thinking about you, Elaine. It is Tuesday the 11th. We have a job meeting every week at that time. I am exploring the News/photo angle. Look forward to meeting you. Bob

[*Bob: Would it be of interest to you to see the cornerstone box that was recovered from the old Roberts Hall? It was a bit of a cautionary tale – a copper box that originally had been soldered closed and then was opened with a crowbar. We had to have someone smooth out the jagged edges, so it wouldn't hurt anyone! Elaine*]

3/10/97
From: Pete Capalongo

Bob:

We will be set to go – brownstone is set to come out – Ugo will be working there this morning if you'd like to check – let me know if there is a change.

Thanks, Pete

To the Coming Man and Woman

March 11 was stormy, the type of weather that Ithacans expect in late winter: blustery, and spitting a cold rain. A small group assembled, including the Sage Hall project management team, led by Bob, artisans from the Cornell Mason Shop, Elaine Engst, David Stewart, and John Gutenberger. Workers had previously dug around the large cornerstone searching for the capsule with no luck. Ugo Spadolini, a master stonemason, dismantled the bricks on the back of the stone but found nothing. As Bob and the others watched, his foreman, Pete Capolongo, chose a drill with a very long bit and drilled high in the stone, still with no luck. Finally, drilling into the middle of the stone, the bit popped through into a large cavity. Feeling around with a coat-hanger, Pete said he could feel documents.

As Bob recalls the event:

The gray, miserable weather suited the underlying sense of dread I felt that day. At the same time, the windy drizzle accentuated the chill of excitement at the unknown thing we were about to uncover. I was in the middle of a difficult project to stuff a modern business school into the delicate historic façade of Cornell University's first residence for women, and little was proceeding as planned. Opening the Sage Hall cornerstone and time capsule to reveal Ezra Cornell's mysterious letter was a diversion from our other troubles, but hardly welcome.

To the Coming Man and Woman

Opening the cornerstone was not a consequence of the construction project, but rather of the curiosity of a student of the Johnson Graduate School of Management who learned of the letter addressed to the "coming man and woman" while researching the history of Sage College and her undergraduate predecessors. Now, a dozen or so modern Pandoras huddled against the weather, most anticipating hope, me worrying about all the things that could go wrong.

What if Pete Capalongo's drill, used to locate the hollow containing the time capsule within the cornerstone, had shredded the Founder's letter or damaged some other historic artifact? What if Ugo Spadolini's electric chisel stabbed through the stone lid and did worse to same? What if Ezra's letter was a curse upon whosoever shall cause the end to this women's college? I imagined the earth opening up, the drizzle worsening to a flood creating a third gorge to split the campus, washing our project away. Would this be covered by our Builder's Risk policy?

Bob felt there was something about this whole exercise that didn't seem right, but that there was no good reason not to proceed.

Bob with the time capsule, March 11, 1997

Photo by Sharon Wargo

To the Coming Man and Woman

The base course of the foundation of the building is Llenroc (Cornell spelled backwards) from a local quarry, the next layer is brownstone, and above that is the water margin, made of Medina sandstone. The masons pulled out the water margin and the red brick above it, revealing a three-inch border around the top of the sidewalls. This was the three-inch-thick stone lid of the lead box, which sat inside the stone, wedged in with hand-cut iron nails, and mortared. The group agreed to meet back at the cornerstone at 1:00, but when that time came Ugo was still working on getting the lid off the box. Trying to cut the lid in half, he had broken a hammer; his helper brought a bigger one, and they finally gained access to the time capsule by cutting off the lid with a grinder. As promised, it did contain a letter signed by Ezra Cornell, and Elaine Engst confirmed that it was written in his neat handwriting, easily distinguished from what she characterized as A.D. White's scrawl.

Elaine stood in the cold wind, reading the letter to the small group, and as she read, all realized what an important find this actually was. To this day, Bob gets choked up just thinking about those still relevant words. In fact, when the University President Hunter Rawlings was informed of the event, he was quite unhappy that he had missed the opportunity to open the time capsule with more fanfare.

However, the Board of Trustees was meeting on campus the next day, and all the materials from the box were placed outside

To the Coming Man and Woman

their meeting room in the Statler Hotel. Ezra Cornell III read his great-grandfather's letter to the Board, as detailed in the *Chronicle*:

Newly unearthed letter affirms Ezra Cornell's commitment to university's Nonsectarianism, by Jill Goetz

> For nearly 125 years, historians have assumed that a letter written by Cornell founder Ezra Cornell and placed for posterity into the Sage Hall cornerstone concerned the university's coeducational status. After all, the campus building was to house the Sage College for Women at the only coeducational institution of higher education in the eastern United States.
>
> But historians could only assume, for Cornell made no copy of his letter and showed it to no one at the time. No one but the author himself knew its contents. Until now.
>
> On Tuesday, March 11, workers renovating the building were able to remove the letter. Dated May 15, 1873, the day of the laying of the Sage Hall cornerstone, the letter is addressed to "the Coming man & woman." Cornell writes:
>
> > *On the occasion of laying the corner stone of the Sage College for women of Cornell University, I desire to say that the principle [sic] danger, and I say almost the only danger I see in the future to be*

To the Coming Man and Woman

encountered by the friends of education, and by all lovers of true liberty is that which may arise from sectarian strife.

From these halls, sectarianism must be forever excluded, <u>all</u> students must be left free to worship God, as their concience [sic] shall dictate, and <u>all persons</u> of any creed or all creeds must find free and easy access, and a hearty and equal welcome, to the educational facilities possessed by the Cornell University.

Coeducation of the sexes and entire freedom from sectarian or political preferences is the only proper and safe way for providing an education that shall meet the wants of the future and carry out the founders idea of an Institution where "any person can find instruction in any study." I herewith commit this great trust to your care.

At an open session of the Cornell Board of Trustees on campus last Friday, President Hunter Rawlings invited Ezra Cornell, a trustee and direct lineal descendant of the Founder, to read the letter aloud. Except for the sounds of clicking cameras, the Statler Amphitheater was utterly silent as trustees, local officials and journalists listened to Cornell softly reciting his ancestor's words from a one-page letter held in a slightly shaking left hand.

To the Coming Man and Woman

"What makes this letter so poignant," said Rawlings, "is that Cornell University at that time was under attack." As he reminded trustees, Cornell was vehemently criticized – labeled "godless" and "infidel" Cornell by preachers, college presidents and the public alike – for its nonsectarian stance, which many people equated with atheism. Though Cornell was not the first university to be nonsectarian, it was perhaps the most conspicuous, and therefore the most berated.

Rawlings quoted from Cornell's remarks at the Sage dedication ceremony all those years ago: "I will close, with the remark that the letter deposited in the cornerstone addressed to the future man and woman, of which I have kept no copy, will relate to future generations the cause of the failure of this experiment, if it ever does fail, as I trust in God it never will."

Written just five years after Cornell's founding, the letter makes clear that that "experiment" was not coeducation – which the founder took as a given, as reflected by the letter's salutation as well as its text – but rather that the freedom of ideas, freedom of access, freedom of worship and freedom of political beliefs should form the essential core of this new university. "An interesting lesson for us in 1997, as well," Rawlings said.

Current trustee Cornell first saw his ancestor's letter on Wednesday. "I have to tell you, it gave me chills," he said. "People have assumed that whatever was in the letter had to do with the experiment of women's education. But this letter proves that the Founder assumed women would be fine on this campus."

He added, "Of all the issues that bothered the Founder in 1873, such as finances, politics, recruiting students and faculty and the equal education of women, it was the subject of religious conflict that he chose for us to read...124 years later. This characteristic of being nonsectarian was one of the important concepts that made Cornell University the first truly American university."

The letter's unearthing is largely the result of lucky timing. Sage Hall, a Victorian Gothic building that served as a women's dormitory from 1875 until World War II and more recently housed the university's graduate school, is being renovated to serve as the future home of the Johnson Graduate School of Management. Cornell officials have long known of the cornerstone's contents but had no definite

To the Coming Man and Woman

plans to remove them. (Cornerstones generally are not opened until a building is demolished.) But about a month ago, Johnson School student Tatiana Rosak read this passage about Cornell's letter in a book by Charlotte Williams Conable: "Cornell's views remain a mystery, enclosed within the walls of Sage College." Intrigued, Rosak approached John McKeown, director of business operations for the Johnson School, asking whether the letter could be retrieved. McKeown, in turn, called University Archivist Elaine Engst to discuss the possibility, and the process of retrieval had begun.

The letter was unearthed with other artifacts on Tuesday, March 11. Four workers spent 45 minutes carefully chipping away at the cornerstone and concrete surrounding the snugly positioned, heavy lead box. Once it had been removed, Engst retrieved its contents and read the letter aloud to students and staff assembled at the site.

"It was amazing," she recalled. "It was very cold, and I was wearing a hard hat; but here I was, the first person reading these secret words aloud." She added, "I thought it was especially nice that that person was a woman."

> Ithaca New York
> May. 15th 1873
>
> To The Coming man & woman
>
> On the occasion of laying the corner stone of the Sage College for women, of Cornell University, I desire to say that the principle danger, and I may almost the only danger I see in the future to be encountered by the friends of Education, and by all lovers of true liberty is that which may arise from sectarian strife, From these halls, sectarianism must be forever excluded, <u>all students</u> must be left free to worship God, as their concience shall dictate, and <u>all persons</u> of any creed, or all creeds must find free, and easy access, and a hearty and equal welcome, to the educational facilities possessed by the Cornell University, Co-education of the sexes, and entire freedom from sectarian or political preferences, is the only proper and safe way, for providing an Education that shall meet the wants of the future, and carry out the founders idea of an Institution where "any person can find instruction in any study" I herewith commit this great trust to your care.
>
> Ezra Cornell

Ezra Cornell's letter "To the Coming Man and Woman"
Courtesy of the Division of Rare and Manuscript Collections,
Cornell University Library

To the Coming Man and Woman

The cornerstone box was officially placed by Mrs. Henry W. Sage (ironically, an opponent of women in higher education) in the presence of assembled dignitaries, including Cornell (who died the following year and never did see the building completed); President Andrew Dickson White; the presidents of several other universities; and members of the Cornell faculty.

Also in the box were the university's first copies of the Register (akin to today's catalog); a pamphlet of the university's laws and documents; a May 5, 1873, copy of the student weekly publication *The Cornell Era*; photos of Mr. and Mrs. Sage; the *Albany Evening Journal Almanac* of 1873; and three newspapers, all dated May 14, 1873: *The Ithaca Journal*, *The Ithaca Daily Democrat* and *The New York Times*. All of the documents are extremely well preserved.

The university plans to place new mementos back into the Sage cornerstone in the next few weeks, Engst said. The lead box and its contents will be archived and put on display in the Cornell Library, she said, adding that Cornell's letter ultimately will be available on the World Wide Web.

During breaks from their meetings on Friday, Cornell trustees viewed the historic letter and other cornerstone

To the Coming Man and Woman

contents in a lobby of the Statler Hotel, in the shadow of the Sage Hall renovations across the street. The trustees themselves reflect the Founder's commitment to nonsectarianism: the Cornell Charter stipulates that at no time can a majority of the trustees belong to any single religious sect.

The trustees clearly were moved by the power of the letter's words and their enduring relevance.

Judith Berman Brandenburg said of the letter, "It reinforced the feeling I had about the kind of advanced thinking that went into the university, that was there from its inception."

Thomas W. Jones observed, "It brought home to me in a more immediate way how truly visionary Ezra Cornell was." He added, "I think he would be very pleased with what he saw today. There is a strong commitment on the part of the board of trustees to uphold Ezra Cornell's vision."

A few months later the project was moving on with plans to reinstall the cornerstone, with a new time capsule.

To the Coming Man and Woman

5/1/97 [*to the project team*]
From: John McKeown

FYI:

I just spoke to Margie Wilson in Sam's [*Johnson*] office, to ask her to let Mr. Johnson know that the Sage cornerstone will now be sealed in the fall, during Trustee/Council weekend (Oct. 15-18), and that we will follow-up with him at a later date regarding the material he would like to have included.

This information regarding the change in date was shared with Tom by Hank Dullea this morning.

Eric – was Hal consulted on the October date? As long as it doesn't mess up any construction details I guess it is OK.

John

[*Hal & Steve: FYI. This is something new to me. We'll have to follow up with the President's office. Eric*]

[*Eric, Steve: I can't say I was consulted on this one, but Hank and I did talk about it quite some time ago. I knew that this was a possibility and I assume Hank took it to the President and he agreed. Any problem accommodating this (I hope the answer is "no", but tell me the truth anyway). Cheers, Hal*]

Bob's reply reflects his level of anxiety regarding the ceremony, and his proactive approach to assuring a good outcome this time around, after the relative fiasco of opening the stone.

5/2/97
From: Bob

Gentlemen:

To the Coming Man and Woman

We have discussed this with Beacon and there are no apparent conflicts. Exterior restoration should be complete. The west step should also be rebuilt. I think we could have a reasonably attractive site on that end of the building. Please let me know if this is a real date and we will make sure the team works toward that goal. Also, if there is some sort of planning committee formed, I'd like to be part of it so that I can both inform the committee and attend to the details the committee would want.

John McKeown expressed the opinion that the project shouldn't pay for this event. "Let the President's Office pay for it." There is much the project must do in the course of completing the work that can be done in a way to support the event. However, I would like some guidance on what is and isn't appropriate to expend with project funds.

I personally feel this is an opportunity for me to support this event with a level of excellence that might atone a bit for my role in the fiasco of opening the cornerstone. Standing by, awaiting my marching orders. I'll do nothing without your knowledge and consent.

Bob

[*Bob - I'd assume for now that the date is real and you should work toward it. As for who pays (this gets tiresome, doesn't it), let's see what's involved before we get too far into that. Hal*]

The ceremony did go forward as planned in October, on a raw autumn day. Meanwhile, a student who would graduate from the Johnson School in 1998 interviewed Bob in late June, and

View from the roof of the Statler Hotel, March 28, 1997
© *Jon Reis Photography*

View from the roof of the Statler Hotel, March 28, 1997
© Jon Reis Photography

To the Coming Man and Woman

wrote a report summing up the progress of the Sage Hall project to date, sending it to Bob for his approval.

Mr. Stundtner,

Below is a draft article regarding the progress at Sage Hall. If there are any inaccuracies, or if you would like to make any changes, please let me know. If possible, I would appreciate it if you could please respond by this afternoon.

Thank you very much for your assistance in preparing this article.

Joe McCusker

[Joe: Good job of distilling my rambling discourse. I've made minor edits in bold and moved some paragraphs, but these are just recommendations. Also, you don't need the "Mr." whether you're quoting me or communicating with me. Stundtner for the former and Bob for the latter works fine. Regards, Bob]

Sage Hall Renovation Back on Schedule, by Joseph A. McCusker

> About ten months ago, Sage Hall's target completion date was in serious jeopardy, according to Robert P. Stundtner, Cornell's Capital Maintenance Project Manager. Creating a modern business school contained in an historic shell is an unusually difficult task in that much of the building is highly irregular. Most of the building shell is neither plumb nor square, according to Mr. Stundtner. It did not help that the structural steel sub-contractor was an antiquated shop that was unable to meet the constant changes and demands of the difficult renovation. The steel sub-contractor delays caused the project to fall three months behind schedule.

To the Coming Man and Woman

Last December, the general contractor had to radically change the planned sequence of work to try to get the job done on-time.

With the workarounds in place, the construction team recaptured two of the three months lost to delays. "We have one month left to accelerate," said Mr. Stundtner, which will be accomplished through employing longer days, weekend time and more laborers. The tight construction labor market in the Ithaca area over the summer led to fewer workers on the job to make up the rest of the lost time. But the Sage Hall workforce increased to 135 workers from 120 over the summer as other construction projects in the area wrapped up. Mr. Stundtner stated that "we want to make up the rest of the time by January, 1998, so that final detail work is done at a reasonable pace." Mr. Stundtner seemed confident that this goal was achievable.

If all goes according to plan, the Johnson School will begin to migrate from Malott Hall to Sage Hall in mid-April, with the entire move completed in early May. The facility should be available for Spring 1998 final exams which begin on May 7. In addition, some of the Johnson School graduation activities are expected to take place in the building. On time completion will allow Sage Hall to be available for Alumni Weekend, and make the June 1998

To the Coming Man and Woman

Twelve Month Option students the first students to attend classes in the renovated facility.

Fortunately, re-allocating space to accommodate the new Parker Center did not create many design or displacement difficulties. The Parker Center lab and trading studio displaced some space allocated to book stacks. Although the library will not be able to accommodate as many books, the Parker Center remains a critical addition to the Johnson School.

Additional project challenges include wiring the building to accommodate the most advanced computer and data distribution technologies. With technology changing at such a rapid pace, the key is to install wiring well in excess of future anticipated capacity. The building will incorporate copper and fiber optic cabling to accommodate the most advanced classroom, desktop and laptop tools.

Mr. Stundtner noted that the Sage Hall project is an interesting business case from two perspectives. From a project management standpoint, the construction team was able to make up a tremendous amount of lost time by changing the sequence of work. Secondly, he thought that it was "amazing how long an inefficient company can remain in business." He called the original structural steel sub-contractor "a model of inefficiency," with nothing computerized, little documentation and an antiquated facility that seemed to employ an overabundance of workers. In contrast, the project's new structural steel sub-contractor uses the latest CAD-CAM and inventory tracking systems, and employs a leaner workforce in its modern facility.

An article in the *Cornell Chronicle* on July 24 revisits the choice of Sage Hall for the new home of JGSM, and details the advantages that the new facility would bring to the school, as well as the major donors that made the building's renovation possible and gave it its name, Sam and Imogene Johnson.

Renovations transform not only Sage Hall but also the Johnson School, by Darryl Geddes

>Having outgrown its current home, Malott Hall, and with an urgent need to upgrade its educational infrastructure, the Johnson Graduate School of Management is spending $38 million to restyle what was once a residence hall for women into a home that will raise its stake in the highly competitive field of awarding MBAs.
>
>Sage Hall, built in 1873, represents the future of the Johnson School and perhaps the future of graduate business education. It will be state-of-the-art in every way: wired

View from the roof of the Statler Hotel, June 27, 1997
© Jon Reis Photography

from floor to ceiling with the latest technology, with a fully operational trading room to mimic those found in Wall Street investment firms and dozens of meeting rooms and spaces for student groups and corporate recruiters. Plans are for the Johnson School to move into Sage Hall by the summer of 1998.

"The building provides us with an advantage among our peer institutions in that it will be a wonderful attraction for incoming students," said Johnson School Dean Robert Swieringa. "But the building is much more than an attraction. It will help us to define what the management education is all about."

To some on campus, the Johnson School is coming to the rescue of Sage Hall, which faced an uncertain future. The building needed upgrades to meet fire and building codes and costly work to repair areas where it had deteriorated. The university studied what to do with Sage Hall for many years without coming to a conclusion until the Johnson School said it would commit millions to renovate the building.

"It really was a perfect solution to the predicament the university faced with Sage Hall," said John McKeown, director of business operations for the Johnson School. "We wanted to stay on central campus and here was this building in need of repair."

The Johnson School, which will gain 60 percent more space in the new facility, is restoring three of Sage's six main exterior walls, removing the interior and digging deeper to create more classroom space. Sage's exterior will get a thorough cleansing. All mortar joints will be replaced, the brick and masonry will be washed and all wood trim restored, refinished and repaired. The spire that stood atop Sage's west tower will be replicated and placed into position by crane. The original spire was destroyed in a storm in the 1940s. Greenhouses, which lined the east side of Sage Hall in its early days, also will be replicated and added on to Sage Hall along East Avenue.

The interior, however, will retain few of Sage's original features. The ground floor will feature seven amphitheater classrooms, student lockers, lounges and student club office space. The first floor will house the Executive Education Center, comprising classrooms and conference rooms and other offices. (Currently the Johnson School's executive education offices are located in guest rooms at the Statler Hotel.)

To the Coming Man and Woman

Administrative offices will be on the second floor along with an expanded career services center with interview rooms. Offices for faculty and Ph.D. candidates, a faculty lounge and seminar and conference rooms will be on the third and fourth floors.

The centerpiece of the new Sage Hall will be a three-story atrium occupying the central courtyard. A skylight, 60 feet by 90 feet, will bathe the atrium in natural light, and glass blocks embedded in the floor will permit sunlight to filter into the basement.

A steel retention system anchored five feet into bedrock supported the exterior walls of the building while the interior was removed during the past year. Inside Sage, the framework of various offices and study spaces is now taking shape. By the end of summer, construction crews hope to have the building "tight" to allow work to proceed indoors during the inclement weather of fall and winter.

"This project has really taken a lot of careful planning and a great deal of engineering expertise to ensure that Sage's exterior walls and mansards were stable enough to withstand the interior work," said Bob Stundtner, the university's project manager.

To the Coming Man and Woman

Giving old Cornell buildings an updated interior is nothing new: Morrill Hall and, currently, Olive Tjaden Hall are two recent examples of such work on campus. The Hillier Group, which was selected to design the new Sage Hall, has managed the restoration of many historic buildings and has designed facilities for other educational institutions. Hillier's lead architect on the project is former Cornell architecture faculty member Alan Chimacoff '64, who as a student designed a piece of concrete sculpture that now stands in the Cornell Plantations.

Alumni and friends of the school have contributed more than $31.5 million toward the project. "Contributions have come from several hundred alumni, giving anything from $5 to $15 million," said Steve Sharratt, assistant dean of external relations for the Johnson School.

The $15 million gift – the largest to date for the project– was given by Samuel C. Johnson '50, for whom the school is named, and his wife, Imogene Powers Johnson '52. Samuel C. Johnson is chairman of S.C. Johnson & Son Inc., also known as S.C. Johnson Wax, one of the world's largest and most successful family-owned businesses.

To the Coming Man and Woman

Johnson School officials have decided to keep the Sage Hall name for the building; other spaces will be named for major benefactors.

"The renovation of Sage Hall is an appropriate metaphor for the Johnson School," said Dean Swieringa. "We're taking the best components of the past and combining them with the best of what the future has to offer. The outcome will benefit and strengthen the Johnson School's award-winning faculty, nationally recognized programs and top-quality students in ways we have yet to realize."

The summer passed by and the weather finally cooperated, with steady progress on the Sage Hall project, and much interest from the Cornell community. Steve Sharratt continued to enlist Bob to help give tours to possible donors and other interested parties.

9/3/97
From: Steven J. Sharratt

Hello Bob:

Your enormous personal magnetism and charisma has created a strong demand for repeat tours of the Sage site. Jeff Parker (trustee, buildings and properties committee member, Sage donor, Parker Center namer, etc., etc., etc.) is in town this coming Friday (9/5) and asked if he could take a late afternoon walk through (4:00 or so). Will that work for you?

To the Coming Man and Woman

I know Sage has become quite a popular campus attraction, and we're getting an increasing number of requests for tours from Day Hall and Brown Road [*Cornell Administration and Alumni Affairs and Development*] as well as from our own current and potential donors. (I haven't heard from the Ladies Auxiliary of the VFW yet, but they should be asking to come through any day now.) Since John McKeown and I know our way around the building fairly well by now, is there a way we can relieve you of some of the tour guiding responsibility? I know you have other things to do. Are there serious liability problems involved in conducting a walk-through without you or a member of your team being present? Please let me know, I don't want these visits to become onerous.

Steve Sharratt

[Steve: Well, I don't know if it's "enormous personal magnetism and charisma" or crazy glue, but you are right about the "other things to do."

I think we should put on the full court press with the CU heavy hitters, even if they have been here before. When available I'd like to help in any way I can. I think we should give Eric [Dicke] a heads up on these people too because he knows many of them and he has his own "enormous personal magnetism and charisma." Crazy glue too for that matter!

Friday at 4ish works for me.

As for the other types of tours, I think you should give John Hermans and me a heads up, check in at the trailer, John and I can come out to greet the guests, apologize for being unavailable to go on the tour (or go or send another as we see fit) and send you on your merry way.

To the Coming Man and Woman

The only caution I think we should make is that if the group is too large (>5+guide), it takes more than one knowledgeable person to shepherd them safely. Besides, who would look out for the falling $$$$'s! Bob]

      Later that month, Bob was consulted for an article about the steeple that had been missing from Sage Hall for 50 years, and the newly fabricated replacement that would be added as part of the renovation. At the time of the article, the Olive Tjaden building on the Arts Quad had just received a replacement steeple of its own.

9/30/1997
To: Bob

I just wanted you to know how much I'd appreciated your taking the time to see me yesterday to discuss steeples for *Cornell Magazine*'s November cover story. We're shipping the issue to the printer in a week, and I'll get copies of the magazine to you just as soon as they're in the office. The story will be in draft stage for another couple days if you have any thoughts to add.

Thanks again for carving time out of your day to see me!

Sharon R. Tregaskis
Assistant Editor, *Cornell Magazine*

[*You are very welcome, Sharon. Get ready for the reopening ceremony next May. This building will knock your socks off when it's done. Regards, Bob*]

To the Coming Man and Woman

Cornell Magazine, November-December 1997
Reared Against the Arch of Heaven, by Paul Cody

The original steeples that crowned Sage Hall and Sage Chapel are, like Tjaden's, long gone. "The chapel steeple was just too large for the building, and was taken down," Kermit Parsons [*Professor Emeritus of Architecture*] says. The steeple atop Sage Hall was removed in 1951 as part of an extensive renovation. It had a wood frame, according to Bob Stundtner, Sage Hall's project manager. "Back then it would have been very hard to scaffold and maintain," he says. "It wasn't maintained, of course, and was removed. I've heard it blew off, though I can't imagine it blowing off and not killing someone."

As part of the Sage Hall reconstruction a new thirty-foot steeple will be added – a concession, Stundtner says, to the Ithaca Landmarks Preservation Committee. "This steeple is a recreation," he says. "We don't have original design drawings, so we've been using historical photos, blowing them up and enhancing them, then taking a look at other details on the building and coming up with a design that we hope will be true to the original." The new Sage Hall steeple, which is expected to cost about $125,000, should be in place by the end of this year. "Knowing the steeple was there, and looking at the building with that knowledge, it looks strange without it," says Stundtner.

"The three stone-row buildings – Morrill, McGraw, White – were built under the direction of Ezra Cornell," Robert Blakeney [*project manager for Tjaden Hall*] says. "He had a very utilitarian view of cost and design, and little sympathy for architecture." But A.D. White, the university's first president, felt that buildings without towers or other aesthetic elements were little more than collections of boxes. "A tower brings a vertical element to a design," says Parsons. "It represents power, which is one of the seven lamps of architecture. It dominates and overwhelms, and it feels, too, as though it might very well fall over on you. But a tower and a steeple also lift the eye, and point upward."

It was around this time in the fall that I visited Bob in the trailer on an errand, bringing him some papers that he had left at home. I found a place to park in the muddy lot, and was walking around the pickup trucks between me and the trailer when I heard a whistle. I've been whistled at before, by construction workers in Paris when I was a teenager for example, but this surprised me as a 40-something woman in jeans and a jacket. I'm sensitive to women's issues, including work-place harassment, and mentioned the incident to Bob as simply a nuisance, but he took it seriously,

To the Coming Man and Woman

noting that in a university setting it's especially important to have clear rules about behavior on construction sites.

Before Bob had devised a strategy to address the problem, his concern was validated. He was giving a tour of the project to Jeff Parker, a university trustee, and his daughter, who was a student in the School of Hotel Administration. In a late program addition to the project, Jeff had given a substantial gift to create an investment and trading center in the renovated Sage Hall. As Bob showed his guests around the project, the daughter commented that she felt uncomfortable walking past the site at lunchtime when the tradesmen would line the construction fence enjoying their lunch and the passing pedestrians.

Recognizing that the workers were creating a hostile atmosphere, Bob requested a mandatory meeting for all the workers on the project, and they assembled in what would become one of the new lecture halls in the basement of Sage. Bob emphasized that Cornell was interested in three things from each person working on the project: to work safely, to deliver the highest quality and to maintain civility at all times. Elaborating on civility, he noted that at Cornell, sexual harassment was defined as a look, a touch or a comment. Beacon continued to emphasize appropriate behavior with their subcontractors and no further complaints were brought to Bob's attention.

To the Coming Man and Woman

Meanwhile, the date for resetting the cornerstone was approaching, and everyone involved hoped that it would go more smoothly than the opening had in March. The president's office sent out a "head's up" in early September.

Subject: TAKE 2 - Cornerstone

Hello, all:

I spoke to President Rawlings this morning and he has chosen the period from 3:30 - 5:00 p.m. on Wednesday, October 15, for the ceremony surrounding the laying of the cornerstone at Sage Hall. Thank you very much,

Amy J. Russ

[*Eric: Take 2 cornerstones and call me in the morning! Hope it's easier to pass this time. Bob*]

Bob consulted with the University Archivist to devise a box for the new time capsule, after John McKeown had sent him Elaine's well-researched suggestions and interesting tidbits regarding industry specifications. Who knew there was an International Time Capsule Society?

To: John McKeown
From: Elaine Engst

Here is some information about "time capsules" I've found from the "archives" of the list-serve for archivists. I'll forward any additional information.

To the Coming Man and Woman

There's a nice Technical Leaflet entitled "The Time Capsule: Repository of the Past or Romantic Notion" available from the American Association for State and Local History – # 182, 1992. And the April 1989 issue of Clemson University's "Clemson World News" (generously sent to me by Michael F. Kohl, Head of Special Collections at Clemson) lists the contents of their Centennial time capsule.

Time capsule enthusiasts have their own organization, the International Time Capsule Society in Atlanta, Georgia.

At least two institutions, Georgia Department of Archives and History and Canadian Conservation Institute, have written guidelines for time capsules.

There is a company in Nampa, Idaho that has manufactured time capsules since 1973. Time capsules vary in size and shape. Most are stainless steel, filled with argon and cost from $1,000 to $4,000.

You might want to consider having all items (paper, photographs, etc.) microfilmed (35mm, silver film, inert plastic reels, acid-free boxes) and enclosed with the originals. A kind of insurance in case something does happen to the originals over time.

Just happened to be looking over the most recent University Products catalogue and on the back cover what should appear but aluminum time capsules in four sizes (with some suggestions on what to and what not to put in them)!

Elaine

To the Coming Man and Woman

Bob was concerned about the costs that Elaine cited, and unsure about whether it would come out of his project budget.

9/10/97
To: Elaine Engst

Hello Elaine:

Pat Redder (sheetmetal shop foreman) and I would like to meet with you to inspect the time capsule removed from Sage last spring. One option would be to reuse the existing box, and I need Pat to look at it and advise us as to whether or not he can repair and re-seal the box.

We're available Monday 9/15 to meet for 1/2 hr anytime between 9:45 am and 1 pm. Can you spare a bit of that day?

Thanks, Bob

[*Bob: Sure - how about 11:15? I don't think that reusing the box would be seen as the best practice. I've found some references relating to time capsules in the "archives" of a list-serve for archivists. I sent them on to John McKeown. If he hasn't forwarded them to you, let me know and I'll send them along. Elaine*]

Elaine:

Pat Redder and I will stop by on Monday at 11:15.

John did forward your e-mail (see his comment below) and I have browsed the web, etc.

[*Bob - I still like the idea of reusing the original box. Can someone in the shops take a look at that option? John*]

While it may not be the best practice, it's not fundamentally different than some of the time capsule offerings I saw out there. I think we

To the Coming Man and Woman

should understand this option so that we have a range of options (and costs) for us to select from.

See you Monday,

Bob

The fallout from opening the cornerstone still troubled Bob, and the following message to his colleagues clearly states his concern over the upcoming ceremony.

9/11/ 97
From: Bob

Gentlemen:

Given what happened the last time I was involved in the cornerstone, I can't help but be increasingly nervous about how the next episode will play out. Some people's e-mails indicate that not everyone in Day Hall knows what's up. I'm pretty certain I don't understand the President's expectations. Who does?

We're a month away from this event and I don't know how many people to expect, how pretty we want to make the site, who pays for anything, etc.

We don't even know what container we'll put back into the void. I'm meeting with the University Archivist Monday morning to review repair/reuse of the existing lead container, but she thinks that isn't a good idea. She referred me to the web to look at products, but my guess is we don't have time for a custom container.

It is not too soon to answer these questions. John McKeown tells me he doesn't have a clue who is "in-charge," but he is meeting with people from Inge's [*Reichenbach, University Vice President*] office on

To the Coming Man and Woman

Tuesday. John will try to make sure we get ourselves into the loop, but I feel like we could have a serious scramble on our hands at the last minute or perhaps scrambled eggs on our faces.

I'll keep you posted on what I can discern. Let me know if you know anything.

Bob

[*Harold D. Craft, Jr.: Bob, In NYC I mentioned this ceremony to Hank Dullea. I believe it's really Hank's show on behalf of the President. Hank said that he would begin to bring this all together. Hal*]

Bob sent out a further message to all those involved, hoping to ward off any problems in advance of the event:

FYI - The President is holding a special ceremony on October 15th, 3:30-5pm to replace the Sage Hall time capsule in the cornerstone. The President, Sam Johnson and other speakers will preside from the mid-landing of the west site-stairs located between the building and Sage Avenue. Guests (scores, perhaps hundreds) will watch from Sage Avenue and possibly the shelter of a tent.

My understanding is that V.P. Reichenbach (Alumni Affairs and Development) is managing the Ceremony planning. I want to make sure that F&CS is prepared to support the event.

This is a heads up (and invitation!) for you, but more importantly, I need a representative from each of your organizations to meet with me next week to discuss the logistics of closing Sage Ave, access to Campus Store, site preparation, security, construction coordination, etc. Please have your representative contact me via e-mail to confirm their availability next Friday.

To the Coming Man and Woman

Thanks,

Bob

  The project team decided to have the Cornell Metal Shop fabricate a new time capsule conforming to the standards of the archival community, a lower cost alternative that could be made a priority to meet the oncoming date of the ceremony.

From: Pat Redder
Subject: Re: Time Capsule for Sage

Hi Sharon [Wargo],

We checked the dimensions of the box and began fabrication accordingly. The size for the acid free box you are having made should be: 12" long x 9-3/8" wide x 4-5/8" deep. Note that these are maximum outside dimensions. Did anyone consider having a jeweler engrave a brass plate to sweat to the top of this?

Pat

[*Elaine & John: Pat has a good idea. What do you think and what should it say? Bob*]

  But there was no time to make up a brass plate; with only days to go, the timetable was tight, as Bob's note to Sharon makes clear.

Sharon:

Please issue two tickets against our SWO# [*standing work order*] for the following.

To the Coming Man and Woman

1) Construct welded stainless steel time capsule for Sage Hall cornerstone. Seal contents in box on 10/15/97 and deliver to Bob Stundtner for ceremony at 3:30pm.

Additional information – Obtain exterior dimensions from Elaine Engst, University Archivist. Provide Elaine the interior dimensions for possible construction of interior acid free cardboard box by CU Libraries. Obtain contents from John McKeown on the morning of October 15th.

2) Remover watertable from cornerstone. At conclusion of ceremony on 10/15/97 3:30 pm, seal cornerstone with stone lid and replace watertable.

Additional information – Obtain previously fabricated stone lid from Bob Stundtner.

Still, Bob's team pulled it off, and a good time was had by all in attendance. *The Cornell Chronicle*, in an article by Darryl Geddes, noted the proceedings and the contents of the new box on October 23rd:

> Now contained within the cornerstone, in a sealed aluminum box, are new letters from Cornell President Hunter Rawlings and trustee Ezra Cornell, a lineal descendant of the university's founder, along with various other items, including a Hewlett-Packard financial calculator, a biography of Samuel Curtis Johnson, for whom the Johnson School is named, and copies of the *Cornell Daily Sun* and the *Cornell Chronicle*.

To the Coming Man and Woman

The cornerstone also contains a copy of the original May 15, 1873, letter from university founder Ezra Cornell, removed from the cornerstone this past spring, in which he discussed the fear that sectarianism would become one of higher education's arch enemies by excluding individuals from a college education based on their religious beliefs.

In his letter, Rawlings writes of a new threat to higher education, and he read the letter at the cornerstone rededication ceremony.

"Today the threat to the university is both more subtle and more pervasive," he read. "A pragmatic public sees the university's primary task as certifying the professional competency of those to whom it awards degrees. Of diminished importance, in the view of many, are a passion for ideas and a commitment to the life of the mind, which are, in fact, the most significant qualities a great university can impart. Credentialism has replaced sectarianism as the greatest threat to higher education, and it must be resisted with equal vigor."

In his letter, Ezra Cornell, the great-great-grandson of the university's founder, continues to caution against sectarianism but notes that Cornell must continue to be

To the Coming Man and Woman

vigilant against "dogmatism and vested interests political, governmental and private in nature." Samuel C. Johnson '50, chair of S.C. Johnson & Son, also referred to as S.C. Johnson Wax, and his wife, Imogene Johnson '52, placed the aluminum box inside the cornerstone shortly before it was sealed with cement. The Johnson School, named for Johnson's great-grandfather, is expected to move into the restyled Sage Hall next spring when the $38 million renovation project – which will provide the school with 60 percent more space and the latest technology – is complete.

Bob's recognition of the members of his project team extends beyond the management component, as witnessed by his thank you to the masons after the cornerstone was reinstalled. Bob comes from the trades himself, having worked with his father as an electrician, and respects the dedication that it takes to be a master craftsman.

10/16/97
From: Bob
To: Pete [Capolongo]:

Thanks for the attention to detail in both uncovering and resealing the time capsule in the Sage Hall cornerstone. I was very pleased to see Ugo Spadolini and Frank Tagliavento standing by at the end of yesterday's ceremony.

To the Coming Man and Woman

We were all nervous about the security of the time capsule and reluctant to leave Sage for the reception at Willard Straight Hall. But once I saw Ugo and Frank, I was more than comfortable to reassure people that the capsule was in good hands.

I especially enjoyed telling Ugo that his photo (noting his name and affiliation) was enclosed in the box. His skill and craftmanship brought the original box safely to light and I think it's a nice touch that he got to seal up the new time capsule, too.

Pete, your shop has brought a great deal of integrity to the construction and preservation of our campus masonry treasures. I'm really glad that you and Ugo got to be so instrumental to this bit of campus history.

Regards,

Bob

During the holiday break of 1997-8, Bob and I went back to Montreal, staying in the same room as the winter before. My mother, sisters and niece were dog- and cat-sitting for us, while Patrick visited his father in Florida. On the morning of our departure from Montreal, we found ourselves outrunning a serious ice storm that would cripple Quebec and northern New York State for weeks. We made it home just ahead of three feet of heavy, wet snow that closed the roads in Tompkins County for 36 hours.

As my father said to Bob on the phone, it was a good thing that we had a lot of wine in the cellar, with all those Cleland women snowed in. We played Blockhead with my niece Justine, a

To the Coming Man and Woman

game that Bob uses for team-building at work. Everyone takes a turn adding a block to the tower until it falls, thus identifying the new Blockhead, who gets to wear a box on her head and start a new tower. The next morning, my mother Jean dug a path through the deep snow to the barn to rescue our cat Tom, who was trapped and crying for help. Wanting to leave as soon as the roads were reopened, "Jean the Machine," as Bob dubbed her, also helped him clear the rest of the driveway before making it safely home to western Pennsylvania.

For my doctoral thesis, I traveled to Cajun country twice between 1992-94 to experience their carnival customs. Their rural practice of chasing chickens through the fields and bringing them back to the village for a communal feast is far removed from the urban celebrations of New Orleans, and closer to the carnival of early modern France where their ancestors had lived before coming to the New World. After the winter break, I taught a second semester of a course based on my dissertation research called "Carnival Cultures." Bob helped me serve my class bowls of homemade gumbo around the same time that he wrote the next Sage Hall progress report. Plans were also moving forward for the installation of the new spire and finial, Sage Hall's crown that had been gone for decades, and was to be recreated and replaced in March of 1998.

To the Coming Man and Woman

Update 15
2/24/98

It's Fat Tuesday and what's more exciting than Mardi Gras? The Sage Hall project!

There's a light at the end of the tunnel and we're the on-rushing train. About 125 workers are putting in long, hard hours six days a week to get Sage ready for the first occupants in mid-April.

The range of work and state of completion spans nearly the entire gamut of trades that have worked on the project. Some rooms are ready for furniture and some don't even have walls, but it looks like we'll get across the finish line successfully. That means we'll be on time, under budget, with the highest level of quality.

Those of you who have toured Sage recently might well wonder how we will ever be on time. The Johnson School will move into their new home over a period of eight weeks. That allows Beacon Skanska Construction to distribute their resources and focus on the rooms needed first.

The Johnson School can't just turn off the lights at Malott Hall one day and turn them on in Sage the next day. For one thing, there's a semester to complete. The faculty, staff, library, computer lab, and various other student support services can't reasonably change facilities right before finals. The train will be leaving the Malott station and arriving at Sage over an extended period of time. Hopefully, the passengers won't have the sense of "missing the train" as a result.

Why wouldn't a project like Sage be under budget? The Trustees approved your budget and you just have to stay within it. Right?

To the Coming Man and Woman

Absolutely. Cost management is one of the most important functions of the project team. But a project of the size, complexity and uniqueness of Sage offers more than the usual suspects for added costs.

Unforeseen conditions are the principal consumer of budget contingencies and at Sage they represent nearly half of the added costs. The unique difficulties of preserving a historic facility while constructing a modern one inside it have exacted a hefty toll.

Another significant source of added cost for many projects is owner directed changes. Often these come from a client who keeps adding to the scope. Every project manager's nightmare is "Scope Creep."

Fortunately for me, the Johnson School has been a model client. While they've been persistent about asking to add some items to the project, in nearly every case they were asking to put back items deleted to meet our original budget. Also, we're trying to invest (prudently) for the long term so we direct upgrades.

At any rate, our current budget projections show us completing the project with sufficient funds left to mop up the muddy footprints and loose threads that every project finds in the end game of project closeout.

When it comes to quality, everybody talks the talk, but not everybody walks the walk. How are we walking the quality walk at Sage? Mainly by adding lots of extra expert eyes to the task.

The design team comes to the site weekly both to answer questions and to monitor compliance to the documents. The contractors have been very committed to meeting the highest standards of their trades. Additionally, we have trades-people from our own shops

To the Coming Man and Woman

meeting regularly with their subcontractor counterparts to review the quality compliance in the field.

Finally, we are implementing a commissioning process to assure the performance of building systems. After confirming the operation of these systems, we're the balancing contractor so we know whether or not the heating, ventilating, and air conditioning systems are delivering the level of performance we paid for. If not, we're in a position to resolve deficiencies quickly.

Notice I didn't say Sage was more fun than Mardi Gras, just more exciting. I'm sure the Johnson School will manage a good bit of fun when they move in. The atrium will be a premier space to have fun in.

We'll have some public excitement next week, morning of March 3rd, weather permitting. The last significant visual change to Sage will be the erection of a historic recreation of the spire that has been missing from the west tower for decades. The spire is poised on a template at ground level on the west side of Sage and it's not too hard to imagine it added 35 feet atop the tower.

The crown jewel will be a 13-foot finial that is another historic recreation of what was perhaps the highest point on any of the early campus buildings. The skilled craftsmen in our own sheet-metal shop created this bronze beauty.

Nearly 50 feet added to the height of Sage. Now that's exciting!

  And the campus community began to anticipate the event:
2/25/1998
From: Kathryn L. Burkgren [*Hal Craft's Assistant*]

To the Coming Man and Woman

Bob – Not to make your life more difficult, but can you (ha, ha) pin down a time when the raising of the spire may take place? Hal would like to be there if possible. If not, that's ok.

Thanks, Kathy

[Kathy: He's not the first to ask. Everyone wants a scheduled time. We're trying to pin it down a bit, but it's just not that scientific. Here's what I'm telling CU news service, etc:

The spire will be erected on the 3rd in the morning. Weather permitting. We need calm winds and no rain. Happens all the time in March! If we get any more precise than that, I'll let you know. It could go very quickly, but I would plan on a long, boring, chilly wait with lousy lighting against the cloudy sky. Bob]

In fact, that's the way it turned out; still, a small crowd of people, including myself, gathered to watch, as reported in the *Chronicle* on March 12.

Sage Hall Reclaims Its Crown Jewel, by Darryl Geddes

> Another Cornell tower has been crowned. In late September last semester, Olive Tjaden Hall's southwest tower was fitted with a new steeple. Last week Sage Hall's west tower was capped with an elaborate re-creation of the spire that adorned it some 50 years ago.
>
> Shortly before 10:30 a.m. March 3, a massive crane lifted the 35-foot spire about 100 feet into the air, where it dangled for more than 15 minutes as workers readied the locking

To the Coming Man and Woman

device inside the tower. About 100 onlookers, who gathered despite the chilly temperatures, applauded as the spire was finally seated on the tower.

"We needed a dry, windless day in March, and we got it," said Bob Stundtner, Cornell project manager. "We also got a bit of drama, plenty of excitement and stiff necks. Everybody here is enjoying another special moment in the history of Sage, the Johnson School and the university."

Once workers securely fastened the spire to the tower, a 13-foot ornate brass and metal finial, designed by Charlie Maira of the Hillier Group and built by Tony Masuta with help from his co-workers in the Cornell Sheetmetal Shop, was placed atop the spire.

Stundtner said designers relied on archival photos to create exact replicas of the spire and finial. "One of our goals in renovating Sage Hall was to pay close attention to its historical nature and to restore the building to what it looked like during its heyday.

"I think the entire renovation of Sage, not just the erection of the spire and finial, demonstrate how dramatically grand this building is again," he said.

To the Coming Man and Woman

Still, some members of the Cornell community questioned the design of the renovation, often citing the disconnect between the old and new parts of the building.

3/5/98
Dear Uncle Ezra,

What made them decide to use a different style of brick for Sage's renovation? It is ugly and very distracting to look at, especially put next to the old Sage bricks. Left wondering at Statler bus stop...

[Dear Left wondering at Statler bus stop...The new façade is different than the old façade because historic preservationists want the new to be readily discernible from the old. Sage Hall is a "Local Landmark" so this was actually a requirement from the Ithaca Landmarks Preservation Committee (ILPC) as a condition for approval of our building permit.

A case in point is the design of the Law School addition. It's collegiate gothic just like Myron Taylor Hall, and uses the same Llenroc stone and slate roof. If that addition had to go through ILPC review today, they would never approve the design. It's too similar to the older building.

At Sage, the new façade uses the "vocabulary" of the historic Sage architecture. Shape and color themes are carried over to the new design, but not literally and with different materials. Red granite is used instead of brick, sheetmetal instead of slate, etc. These themes are even carried into the interior design.

View from the roof of the Statler Hotel, February 26, 1998
© Jon Reis Photography

To the Coming Man and Woman

The barrel-roofed structure is a reference to the greenhouse that used to be in that location. It also serves to transition from the four story 1895 addition at the northeast end of Sage to the two story headhouse at the southeast. The new tower serves as an exclamation point for the transition.

The restoration of the historic façade has been in keeping with the existing materials and even missing elements. We've replaced decorative wood, slate and metal elements that have been missing for decades.

The restored spire on the west tower is the best example. It's as accurate as we can make it based on historic photos. The slate roofing shingles are even from the same quarry as existing slates.

Sage Hall will be fully occupied by the end of May so stop by and walk through. I think the attention to detail will impress you. Regards, Bob Stundtner, Sage Hall Project Manager]

Sidewalk supervisors, as Bob likes to call the critical public, kept close track of the developments at Sage, including this inquiry regarding the new finial:

03/26/98
Dear Uncle Ezra,

Is the rod on top of Sage crooked? It appears to be bent in the east direction.

Or maybe it's just my eyes...

Crook

To the Coming Man and Woman

[*Dear Uncle Ezra & Crook: The east/west centerline of Sage Hall nails the finial at its base, right on. However, the rod is off about 2" to the north at it's top. We think Crook is right about a bit of drift to the east, too. We're not quite sure why, but intend to find out.*

The finial is 22 feet long with 13 feet exposed. It's a 1.25 inch stainless steel rod with a 2 inch bronze pipe plug welded to it. Then decorative .5 inch bronze rods with flowers or stars at the ends are wound around and branch off from the shaft. It was acid etched to give it a patina.

The finial was hand crafted by Tony Musuta, Al Konz and Bob Sents in the Cornell Sheetmetal Shop. Foreman Pat Redder is convinced their finial is as straight as an arrow.

So what could it be? The finial was threaded down through the restored spire and bolted within it. A very tiny misalignment in the spire where it fastens 110 feet up on the west tower probably wouldn't catch the eye, but telescoped across the slender length of the finial it becomes noticeable. The same could happen at the point where the finial is bolted.

We're running full out on the Sage project right now as we finish up for the new occupants. That's why it took us so long to answer Crook's inquiry. Next small break we get, we'll continue the investigation. Stay tuned! Bob]

Few artifacts from the old building were worth saving, an indication of how rundown Sage Hall had become over more than a century of use. Bob sent Elaine Engst and Peggy Haine a message about what to do with some findings from the original building. As usual, Peggy had plenty of ideas…

To the Coming Man and Woman

3/31/98

Peg:

Hillier and I walked the building just before asbestos removal started in May '96 to select interior items for salvage. It was surprising to me that so little was of any interest. We did set aside a few items:

door hinges and knobs

pressed tin ceiling panels

light fixture from Dining

leaded glass windows

square spindles from stairs [*Bob had suggested using them as graduation batons, but the idea had been rejected*]

I asked John McKeown if he could conceive of any use in the building and he referred me to you. What do you think?

Bob

[*Bob: I'm delighted to be asked.*

Of course, Elaine should have first dibs for the Archives. But there was some talk awhile ago of putting together a permanent exhibit honoring women at Cornell in the Sage atrium. Could any of these be used in constructing that exhibit? Are door hinges and knobs brass, iron, or what? Possible to have some artist recycle them into a sculpture?

Would it constitute sacrilege to knock these items off at a benefit auction, perhaps for the Breast Cancer Alliance or some other women-related charitable organization, for the DeWitt Historical Society, the Cornell Archives, or scholarships for Cornell women? Would we want

To the Coming Man and Woman

to do this at reunion (probably too late for this year, but, heck, they're not going anyplace)?

As for the square spindles, Dan Krall (Prof. in the Dept of Landscape Architecture) uses such things to fabricate huge and fanciful birdhouses, which he sells off on behalf of Hospicare for hundreds of dollars at their annual birdhouse auction.

Was there only one light fixture? And if nobody wants those leaded glass windows, I'd like a crack at them. I have the perfect spot...Cheers! Peg]

You sure are good at spinning out great ideas, Peg!

The short answer is yes to most of it with some caveats. My baton idea was shot down because of the notion of creating sacrilegious trophies so I suspect that sensitivity needs to be addressed. Time or Novocain perhaps.

The fixture is being used in the "historic room" on the first floor.

As for personal use of the windows . . . my guess is the line will be long!

Bottom line is these items are available and the historic display is probably the safest use, but certainly not the only option.

If you're working actively with Cynthia and Elaine, perhaps the best thing is to take a look.

Bob

  Peg was right about the findings not going anywhere; as far as we know, the items remain in storage to this day...

To the Coming Man and Woman

4/1/98

From: Sean Copeland [*an undergraduate reporter*]

Hi, I talked to you the other day about the article I'm working on for Friday's paper about Sage Hall for the *Cornell Sun*. I forgot to ask one question. What's the structure with the round roof on the east side? Why does it look like that? What will it be used for?

Thanks,

Sean

[*That's the conservatory. It's where Col Mustard killed Prof Plum with the lead pipe! OK...would you believe there used to be a greenhouse at that location? The general shape and roof pattern is meant to look like glass panes. It also serves to transition from taller structures to the north of the new tower (witch's hat, an exclamation point on a building of towers) to the residential scale head-house (so called because it served as the location where potting soil was mixed for use in the greenhouse). The conservatory will be the reference room of the library.*]

On April 24, Bob and I were married in a small ceremony at our home on Spencer Road. The challenges of the Sage Hall project were slowly winding down, but as the deadline for occupying the building loomed closer, the furniture contractor went bankrupt, requiring another scramble by the project team to find a replacement. A few weeks later Bob wrote another project update, reflecting the elated state of a man who got married, became a parent for the first time, and turned 50, all within a week.

The Conservatory and the east tower "Witch's Hat"

Photo by Jennifer Cleland

To the Coming Man and Woman

Update 16
5/19/98

We have our Temporary Certificate of Occupancy and the first residents have moved in! It's a whirlwind of activity here at Sage Hall as up to a hundred and fifty workers give their best to make ready for Graduation weekend. We're all very excited about what has been accomplished and how great Sage is looking.

One of the many great pleasures of working on the Sage Hall project has been the opportunity to see tradespeople rise up to the challenge of the design. No doubt about it, The Hillier Group, our architects, presented the construction team with a very high standard in terms of degree of difficulty and level of quality necessary to do justice to the design details.

Not every tradesperson who set foot on the project site was up to the challenge and those who weren't were let go. Most gave true meaning to "workmanlike manner" and many stepped up to the challenge as exceptionally skilled craftspersons and even artisans. Two of the PDC Shops' finest exemplify what I'm trying to express.

Various PDC tradespeople are supporting the Quality Assurance and Commissioning efforts of the project. The Mason Shop and the Sheetmetal Shop have also contributed proudly to the finished work.

I've been a rockhound all my life. I can't resist a neat fossil or beautiful stone unless it's too big to carry and gratefully most of what I like falls into that category. One of the things I really like about Cornell is the extensive use of local stone in our buildings and grounds, and stone mason-extraordinaire Ugo Spadolini knows how to work it better than any other in my experience.

To the Coming Man and Woman

At Sage Hall, we had a modest budget set aside to repair a dilapidated set of site stairs leading up to the west entrance on Sage Avenue. Our budget was too tight to afford to do the right thing – replace the stairs. Through a very positive collaboration with Maintenance Management, Jeff Lallas took over the task, supplemented our budget with the necessary resources and recreated the stairs in all their glorious detail.

All winter long, Ugo and his colleagues toiled away under a tent to assemble some of the most beautiful sandstone you'll ever lay eyes on. It was hard to pass by their tent without lifting the flap and taking a peak at how things were going. There was a constant buzz among the construction team about how great the stairs looked.

Finally the work was complete and the tent came down. "Breathtaking" is the only way to describe what was revealed. The sharp detail of the stone and the sensual sweep of the walls only came to light as the result of Ugo's skilled workmanship and experienced understanding of the material. Once more he had worked his magic and created another handcrafted gem on a campus of natural treasures.

Sometimes we toil for years, producing excellent work that only a few truly appreciate. We're all keenly aware of the comfort level of offices and meeting spaces we work in, but few have much appreciation for the skills necessary to fabricate and install the ductwork necessary to achieve a comfortable environment. Tony Musuta is one of the unsung "tin knocker" heroes who long ago achieved well-deserved respect from his colleagues. Then an unusual little project landed on his worktable.

To the Coming Man and Woman

One of the concessions made in the course of obtaining the approval for Sage Hall renovation was a historic restoration of the spire on the west tower, gone for some fifty years. Unhappy with the cost and schedule constraints of proposals from "art" shops, I challenged Pat Redder's Sheetmetal Shop to build a bronze finial to sit on top of the restored spire. Tony Musuta, with assistance from Al Konz and Bob Sents, got the opportunity to show off his architectural skills.

Rarely have I seen anyone get so excited about what they were doing. Tony researched, he mocked up designs, he patiently made adjustments at the architect's request, in short, he got into it! Those aware of what was afoot made regular pilgrimages to the shop to marvel at what was being created.

On a chilly March morning, the 35 foot spire was lifted 110 feet up to the top of the west tower. Finally, it was time to hoist Tony's handiwork to top it all off. As nervous as an expectant parent and grinning from ear to ear, Tony got to revel in the cheers of the small crowd of guests as his whimsical cap of Sage leaves was placed atop the 13 foot finial. The crown jewel was restored.

Not many of the people who climb the beautiful Sage Hall site stairs and look up at the graceful finial will know the names of the artisans who created them, but all will appreciate what was done and how well it was done. We're lucky because we know Ugo Spadolini and Tony Musuta, and even luckier because they are our co-workers.

Bob

[*Shirley K. Egan: Bob – Many thanks for the lively and touching update. I didn't know you were a fossil hound, too. Shirley*]

[And now that I'm fifty I can start to think about being a fossil!]

To the Coming Man and Woman

[*Dear old Bob – Hmm... let's see, if he can be adequately described and distinguished (the former tough, the latter easy), and an example placed in the PRI [Paleontological Research Institute] Type Collection, then he could be named* anageaprojectorus stundtnerii.]

[*And my Latin teacher thought it was Robertus!*]

[*From: Ed Franquemont [Executive Director, Historic Ithaca]: Thank you Bob for the memo. I wonder if we could publish excerpts in our newsletter as many of our members have followed developments anxiously.*

You write so eloquently of the parts of the process seldom seen but so important to the success of a project like this. Of course we'll send our edits for your approval. Regards, Ed Franquemont]

[Ed: I'm really pleased that Historic Ithaca is feeling good about the outcome at Sage. We certainly remember who stood by us in the approval process. Bob]

By coincidence, Ed's construction company had won the bid for an addition to our house a year and a half earlier, and we enjoyed getting to know him better. He was also an expert in Peruvian textiles, and recognized some weavings that I had brought back from South America in 1974 when the Highwoods toured there on a cultural exchange tour. We were sorry to hear that Ed passed away in 2004.

As the public began to use the new building, yet another inquiry to Uncle Ezra concerned the layout of Sage Hall and access to the roof.

To the Coming Man and Woman

7/22/1998

Dear Uncle Ezra,

I would like to know how to get to the top of the new Sage Hall. I've wandered around the 4th floor and didn't see any stairs to get me higher.

Looking for Views

[*Dear Looking For Views, thanks for giving me another opportunity to contact Bob Stundtner, Project Manager for (among other things) the Johnson Graduate School of Management/Sage Hall Renovation, who abounds with interesting information. Bob says that the fourth floor of Sage is the highest occupied floor. Above that it's the various roofs with maintenance access only:*

Although the tower over the west entrance looks like you could get higher, you can't. The highest level of the tower that you can get to is actually a faculty lounge on the third floor. Like many of the spaces in the revitalized Sage Hall, this lounge is quite unique. In this case the room is over two stories high. You can look into it from the fourth floor corridor.

The ceiling of the lounge is a fire-rated structure that protects the wood timbers and framing of the tower roof. It's so high that it actually blocks off the old doorway that provided access to the upper tower. The door is still there, but there's a block wall on the other side of it.

There is very little to see or do once in the highest reaches of the tower, and it will take scaffolding to gain access for maintenance purposes.

View from the roof of the Statler Hotel, June 1, 1998
© Jon Reis Photography

To the Coming Man and Woman

My favorite views in Sage Hall are the window in the northwest stairs between the second and third floors, the little reading room (old porch) in the northeast corner of the building overlooking East Avenue and the Statler, and the second floor overlook on the Atrium. Can you identify the architectural reference between this overlook and the old porch? Enjoy! Thanks, Bob]

Even with the big problems solved, any project has issues up to and including the final punch list; but no one expected trouble with the locks in the brand new building. Two more Cornell craftsmen came to the rescue:

To: The Locksmith's – Mike Hingston, Mike Aug & Bill Miller

From: Bob

Thanks for all your tweaking, adjusting, detective work, etc.

Sharon and I both breathed a sigh of relief when Mike Aug finally figured out the strange case of the keys that wouldn't work. Mike determined that the manufacturer and the vendor had goofed and created a royal pain for the Sage team when many people couldn't get their keys to open the doors. It wasn't the key logic that Mike and Sharon had created after all. How could we have ever doubted?

Mike Hingston and Bill Miller went through every door in the building creating a punch-list. Their fame as locksmiths was so renowned that the contractors also hired them to correct the defects on the fly whenever possible. Some of the items will take a bit more work to correct, but our guys created another win/win situation for all involved.

To the Coming Man and Woman

Thanks for keepin' 'em honest, guys! Sharon may have more to say about this.

Regards dear friends,

Bob

An article in the *Chronicle* on August 13 continued the public's education about national guidelines regarding historic preservation, and the specific references that Alan Chimicoff's architectural team had made to Charles Babcock's design for the original building.

Historic References Link Renovated Sage Hall With Its Past, by Justine Dougherty

> Giving a tour of the building, Bob Stundtner discussed the ways in which the aesthetic elements of the old and new portions blend. "The modern additions use the vocabulary of the older building," he said, "respecting but not replicating it. It's not note for note but more like a jazz riff – the feel of the song is there."
>
> Stundtner pointed out some of the areas in which this referential system is in evidence:
>
> - The new triangle windows facing East Avenue make reference to the older gable end dormers.

To the Coming Man and Woman

- The cut of the new front entrance, on East Avenue, is in reference to the shape of the older south entrance.

- The granite that clads the new exterior, though not the same color as the older bricks, shares the same color warmth and will match them as the old bricks lose their clean shine.

- The Rheinzink (sheet metal used for roofing) was cut and laid to imitate the patterning of the glass on one of the old greenhouses – now library reading rooms – on the southeast corner.

- The exposed steel buttresses in the atrium (decorative rather than structural) point to when the building was first built: during the height of the Industrial Revolution.

- The new brick walls in the atrium are ribbed with steel control joints to make the façade look modular and therefore more modern in assembly.

There are also other additions that are indirectly related to the past. For instance, the terrazzo tiles in the atrium match the floor pattern in the Sage Chapel crypt, and the tops of the carrels in the new library are rounded like chapel pews,

To the Coming Man and Woman

both alluding to the fact that Sage Hall and Sage Chapel were designed by Cornell's first professor of architecture, Charles Babcock, and built at the same time.

Bob's final project update recapitulates his experience of the renovation from beginning to end, from the initial need to save the building from further deterioration to the highlights and low points of the process that created the new home for the Johnson Graduate School of Management. Ezra Cornell's letter "To the Coming man and woman" figures as the pivotal moment, both physically and psychologically, for the successful conclusion of the transformation of Sage Hall, and reminds us of the touchstone for Ezra's educational philosophy: that any person, regardless of sex, race or religious affiliation, was welcome to study at Cornell University.

Update 17
9/20/98

It's the Autumnal Equinox. Night and day are in balance. Sage Hall seems to be in balance, too. The old and the new, our history and our future seem perfectly in balance to me.

What a marvelous building the revitalized Sage Hall is. I know the renovation was controversial in some quarters. Many feared the loss of the "history," but for me this project has meant the discovery of the story, its revelation, its reinterpretation, and the writing of new chapters of an enduring saga.

My discovery of Sage began in the spring of 1996. Bonne Wagner,

To the Coming Man and Woman

construction administrator for The Hillier Group, and I were surveying the building to identify historic elements to be salvaged.

It was an unseasonably hot day as we started at the top of the west tower and worked our way down through the mostly abandoned building. I think we both sensed the passing of an era. The mournful chirp of smoke detectors randomly announcing their dying batteries reminded us that Sage had started as and only recently ceased to be a residence hall.

Sadly, there was very little that was left of the original building finishes. Numerous renovations over the past century had erased the truly old. By the time we made our way to the furthest basement recesses, we were thoroughly disappointed with how short our list was.

One bright spot was a chandelier we found hanging in Sage Dining that also appears in very old photos of the parlor on the first floor. This and other items (pressed tin ceilings, door hardware, leaded glass windows) were carefully packaged and placed in storage.

As the removal of asbestos containing plaster progressed that summer, more of the story was revealed. Structurally, Sage was a deeply wounded building. Wood truss systems were used in three locations to create large open spaces on the first floor. Each had failed and each had undergone multiple attempts at repair.

The failure of the five trusses in the center south portion of the building was so extensive that the north wall of the space was noticeably bulged outward and buttresses were added in the courtyard around the turn of the 20th century. When the plaster was removed from the walls and ceilings, the remaining restraints to total collapse were removed and the wall shifted eighteen inches in one morning. We spent five days analyzing how to safely brace the structure so as not to damage the south wall that was to be incorporated into the renovated Sage.

When Sage first opened, it offered the occupants the latest in amenities such as indoor plumbing including hot water, steam heat and gas lights. The plaster removal revealed the evolution and expansion of technology and safety features.

The first significant change was the introduction of electric lighting and I'll bet the chandelier we salvaged was one of the first fixtures to be installed. Subsequent expansions of electrical service caused significant structural damage as more and more circuits were added to meet growing demands from occupants.

The expansion of restrooms and the introduction of hot water heat and a sprinkler system also contributed to a degradation of the structural integrity. More than one structural engineer touring the exposed structure remarked that Sage probably would have been condemned had anyone realized how shaky some areas were.

In the course of the selective demolition and excavation the swimming pool was finally uncovered. I'd call it a wading pool and one can imagine that in 1895 women's bathing suits probably discouraged actual swimming.

I was never able to confirm one enduring campus myth. We found absolutely no evidence that horses had ever been residents of the basement. Although some of the rooms looked like animal stalls, the low ceilings could only have accommodated the smallest of ponies.

We had to excavate twenty feet below the old basement level to create useful space in the renovated Sage. In the eastern end of the

To the Coming Man and Woman

excavation, the bedrock was higher than anticipated and I glimpsed many interesting fossil layers, but the pace of work was feverish and there was no time to study that bit of history.

By New Year's Day 1997, the deconstruction of Sage had ended. From the outside, Sage looked unchanged except for the strange exoskeleton encircling it. But walking through the new tunnel entrance at the southeast corner of the building you stepped out into the awesome sight of five story walls and mansard roofs draped in bright red tarps encircling the excavation with the bright blue winter sky above.

A couple of weeks later, the first of the structural steel arrived and the reconstruction began. We were two months behind schedule, and what already seemed a feverish construction pace had to be become furious if we were to meet the May '98 beneficial occupancy commitment.

Our contractor, Beacon Skanska, had to regularly adjust the construction sequences as the steel subcontractor continued to miss delivery schedules. The challenge was made all the more difficult as the construction boom expanded throughout the northeast. Skilled trades resources were scarce, so overtime became a requirement to keep the possibility of finishing on time alive.

At times, our prospects for success seemed as miserable as the weather, but we found inspiration in a key element of the Sage Hall "story." On Tuesday, March 11, we uncovered the cornerstone time capsule containing a mysterious letter written by Cornell founder Ezra Cornell.

Historians had long speculated that the letter concerned the university's coeducational status because the building was to house

To the Coming Man and Woman

the Sage College for Women at the only coeducational institution of higher education in the eastern United States. I personally feared we'd find some version of the mummy's curse and the walls would collapse when we unsealed the capsule. "Beware the Ides of March," I recalled, and the 11th seemed close enough.

We stepped into the west entrance to get out of the chilling drizzle as Elaine Engst, University Archivist, unfolded the letter addressed to "The Coming man & woman," and softly read aloud:

"On the occasion of laying the corner stone of the Sage College for women of Cornell University, I desire to say that the principal danger, and I say almost the only danger I see in the future to be encountered by the friends of education, and by all lovers of true liberty is that which may arise from sectarian strife.

"From these halls, sectarianism must be forever excluded, all students must be left free to worship God, as their conscience shall dictate, and all persons of any creed or all creeds must find free and easy access, and a hearty and equal welcome, to the educational facilities possessed by the Cornell University.

"Coeducation of the sexes and entire freedom from sectarian or political preferences is the only proper and safe way for providing an education that shall meet the wants of the future and carry out the founders' idea of an Institution where 'any person can find instruction in any study.' I herewith commit this great trust to your care."

We felt that the project was entirely consistent with the Founder's wisdom and that the revitalized Sage Hall would be further proof that his fears were not realized. It was a spiritual turning point for us and fortified us for what sometimes seemed a daunting task.

To the Coming Man and Woman

By summer '97, the building addition was taking shape. Slowly at first, but even the sidewalk superintendents became excited, especially as the granite façade and Rheinzink roof were being installed.

The interior spaces were also being delineated. Although stuffed with scaffolding and dimly lit, the Atrium was obviously going to be a spectacular public space. During a tour, Sam Johnson, JGSM's principal benefactor, and Harold Tanner, Cornell Board of Trustees Chairman, realized the Atrium would make a rather dramatic venue for dinner parties – and they were right. President Rawlings hosted the first such event the night before Commencement last spring.

This will be my last Sage Hall Update. I'm in balance between the old challenge and the next challenge.

Bob

Epilogue

Bob would be the first to point out that the successful outcome of the Sage Hall project came from collaborations among many people, who contributed good faith efforts to produce a result larger than their own fields of expertise. But perhaps the most important unforeseen condition of any project is also the human element – the people who make up the team, and the life changes that inevitably occur in the course of several years.

The most obvious example for Bob is his divorce and remarriage during the renovation. Patrick and I moved in with him in May of 1997; we started an addition to the house around Thanksgiving of that year, and drank our wedding champagne in the new dining room in April of '98.

But some key members of the Sage project team were challenged by tragic events. Two people were diagnosed with cancer, and one of them died; one person's father died in a car accident, and then his mother had a heart attack and died when she identified the body. One man's new wife committed suicide soon after they married, and he spent time in recovery after his alcohol use became a problem. Life is what happens while we're making other plans...

This story of success also concerns conscious evolution. Bob benefited from Cornell's Leadership Development Program,

Epilogue

initiated by Hal Craft in the Facilities Services Department, and expanded in the decades since to the larger Cornell staff as the Harold D. Craft Leadership Program. Bob's own path to leadership was guided and shaped by his participation in the program, and its influence is reflected in all of his project reports; most explicitly in his final message, Bob expresses his gratitude for his own and his partners' growth in the course of the Sage project and their careers at Cornell University. He wrote this last report in the fall of 1998:

'So what are you working on now, Bob?' That's what everybody asks.

Just because the Johnson School has moved in and they've dedicated the building doesn't mean the project is done. Lots of mopping up to do after spending so much money. You just can't help but spill a bit here and there!

For instance, I just authorized the last $15,000 payment to Gilbane Building Company for the Baker/Olin project and substantial completion was two years ago. Our dear friends at Johnson Controls were struggling with delivering a small bit of software and I was too stubborn to let them off the hook. Here's hoping that Beacon and their 50 subcontractors understand how stubborn I can be!

I'm back in my old Maintenance Management stomping grounds in Humphreys after eight years out in the field. It's good to be back with my Facilities colleagues and to have a chance to reflect a bit.

Since 1991, I've spent over $60 Million. And you wonder why I don't have any hair!?! I've been very fortunate to have led teams on two of the most challenging projects in the last decade. Of course, just

Epilogue

about everything we do here at Cornell is more challenging than the last thing we did.

The most challenging and satisfying work that I've done in all that time was to supervise Sharon Wargo and Paul Sarokwash. Actually, I came to call the meetings I had with them "Duovision" to more accurately reflect what was happening. We were supervising each other.

By that I mean the process was so mutually beneficial. I learned to delegate, give and receive feedback, and recognize accomplishments – and so did they. We all grew in our relationship with each other and as a result became more effective managers of our "tasky" responsibilities.

Some of our interpersonal success was due to what each of us brought to the table originally. We're bright, funny, hardworking people who became committed to each other in the course of working together. I'm sure we could have survived quite nicely on just that sort of good will that most people bring to the table.

But we were luckier than that. I believe that the cultural changes in F&CS had the most profound effect on our relationships. As a supervisor, I was the first to get exposed to LDP and because we were already so close Sharon and Paul made it easy for me to take the lessons to heart. I might stumble now and then, but they provided a supportive environment to get back on track.

Eventually, Sharon and Paul also went through LDP, and my little staff really started to click. Now, they're both off to new positions with supervisory responsibilities of their own, Sharon as Manager of Operations for University Libraries and Paul as Director of Public Works for a small township north of Philly.

Epilogue

To Sharon and Paul: Thanks for all your support. May you find as much satisfaction in being a supervisor as I did in being yours. Congratulations! Best wishes! I love you and I'll miss you, but not too much because you'll always be a part of who I am.

Bob

As for Bob and me, we're still praising the goddess of mercy for our love. I got to be the project manager for the renovation and addition to our cottage on Spencer Road, and I still play Irish music. Bob went on to manage the construction of Duffield Hall, the nanotechnology lab built on campus from 2001 to 2004, before becoming the Director of Capitol Project Management at Cornell, and he still collects fossils. And, essential to our family unit, Bob has been an engaged and loving parent. Patrick even followed in his stepfather's footprints, graduating *Magna Cum Laude* with a bachelor's degree in Philosophy and Psychology from SUNY Oswego in 2007, and currently lives in San Francisco.

We have enjoyed assembling this personal and professional account of the history of Sage Hall, and hope it will be of interest to the Cornell community, students of women's struggle for equality, and, of course, modern project managers.

Bibliography

Becker, Carl, <u>Cornell University: Founders and the Founding</u>, Ithaca: Cornell University Press, 1943.

Bishop, Morris. <u>A History of Cornell</u>. Ithaca: Cornell University Press, 1962.

Coit Ellicott, Ellen. <u>It Happened This Way: American Scene</u>, Burlingame, California: Privately printed by Beejay Press, 1987.

Comstock, Anna. <u>The Comstocks of Cornell</u>, Ithaca: Cornell University Press, 1953.

Kammen, Carol. <u>Part and Apart: The Black Experience at Cornell, 1865-1945</u>, Ithaca: Cornell University Library, 2009.

<u>Margaret Milmoe Papers, 1886-1924</u>. Cornell University Archives.

Parsons, Kermit. <u>The Cornell Campus</u>, Ithaca: Cornell University Press, 1968.

Ruskin, John. <u>The Stones of Venice</u>. New York, Hill and Wang, 1964.

Sachs, Daniel. <u>The Origin and Early Years of Coeducation at Cornell University, 1955</u>. Cornell University Archives.

<u>Autobiography of Andrew Dickson White</u>, Ithaca: Cornell University Press, 1905.

Authors

Robert P. Stundtner was born in Rochester, NY in 1948. He graduated Magna Cum Laude from SUNY Oswego. When he isn't warping space and time, he tries to make a difference. He is most successful in his endeavors when he adheres to his personal and professional values of truth, respect, teamwork, excellence and integrity.

Jennifer Cleland was born in Arlington, VA in 1951. Her family moved to Europe in 1962, where they lived in Paris and in Stuttgart, Germany. During the 70's, Jenny played with the Highwoods Stringband, touring on three continents and receiving a Grammy nomination for an album recorded at Carnegie Hall. She received a Ph.D. in Romance Studies from Cornell University in 1999 with her thesis *Cajun Carnival: American Myths and Radical Roots*.

While we are traveling the world together, you can contact us at sagehallbook.com or via our LinkedIn profiles.

www.ingramcontent.com/pod-product-compliance
Lightning Source LLC
Chambersburg PA
CBHW071648090426
42738CB00009B/1460